Lyra McKee was born in 1990 in Belfast. She won the Sky News Young Journalists Award in 2006 and became an investigative reporter, writing for numerous newspapers, magazines and w   She was featured as one of the Forbes 30 under 30 and a
        :ary star by the *Irish Times*. McKee was fatally shot during
   . Derry in 2019. At the time of her death, she was working
   ce of investigative journalism entitled *The Lost Boys*, which
   et ready for publication but remains under review with
   id those closest to her.

praise for Lyra McKee and *Lost, Found, Remembered*:

l and trusted champion of the lost, marginalised and those, self, who have suffered growing up in a discriminatory ament . . . a brilliant flame extinguished.' Patti Smith

'[I   was a] powerhouse . . . and since her death she has pulled
o   ore than she could ever have expected by bringing all
      unities together.' Anna Burns

ι   con for Northern Ireland . . . Public Lyra was a brilliant
j.   ist and advocate; someone who spoke up for others and
fea   ily probed at uncomfortable subjects. The Lyra I got to
kno   was upbeat and kind; a devoted carer to her mother.' Sinéad
Gle   1

'Ly   cKee was one of us. She was our people. She didn't think
she   , not at first – Belfast isn't the easiest place in the world to
gro   o gay – but she found a way to belong here, a way to tell her
sto   he was our people because that includes a lot now, and it
inc   d her. It's not like it used to be. But it doesn't include them,
no   more. Whatever you say, say that.' Paraic O'Donnell

'N   vas a young writer who could reach into the eerie spaces of
w   d happened to us before she was born, to know the things
th   ited us.' Eoin McNamee

'Lyra transcended boundaries with her humanity, compassion and curiosity.' Ruth Dudley Edwards

'Lyra McKee represented a future, another country, a better one.' Martin Doyle, *Irish Times*

'Lyra McKee was willing to look fearlessly at the worst flaws in the North while never losing a sense of hope for the place. Reading this collection of the late Lyra McKee's work can be a painful experience. Not because of the writing, which is humane and curious, but because of the reader's ever-present knowledge of what happened to the author . . . McKee's writing career was going somewhere and her contribution would surely have been significant . . . A year on from her death, the talent evident in this volume does nothing to leaven the senselessness of her death – instead it draws even starker attention to it.' Matthew O'Toole, *Irish Times*

'McKee defied her upbringing in a closed-off, no-go area by greeting the world with a radical openness . . . Despite its slim size, this volume is a monumental parting gift by McKee that tells us more about her and about Northern Ireland. It is a place for which she exhibited enormous love and hope, and her stance is one that we must follow to ensure that, as she predicted, "it's going to get better". Let this be her legacy, and ours.' Dawn Miranda Sherratt-Bado, *Dublin Review of Books*

'The enduring lesson of Lyra McKee's life is that an individual can make a difference. The enduring lesson of her death is that journalists determined to act as witnesses to history, running towards the sound of gunfire, take the ultimate risk.' Roy Greenslade, *Guardian*

'A young journalist and LGBT activist whose campaigning life and tolerant, progressive outlook stood in direct contrast to the violent nihilism of those that had taken it . . . In death, Lyra McKee became an icon, a symbol of a young Northern Irish demographic.' Sean O' Hagan, *Observer*

'Lyra McLee was a one-woman union for the reputation of journalism . . . There was no pretended objectivity with Lyra. She was for the poor, the minorities, the refugees, the sex workers, the abused and all those left behind in a country struggling to catch up with a promised but elusive future . . . [*Lost, Found, Remembered* is] brimming with the oversized talent and boundless potential of a woman who never saw thirty but crammed the lives of one hundred journalists into her short life . . . If you have come to view journalism with contempt, if you are convinced it's all rotten and corrupt and ephemeral, you still have to reckon with Lyra McKee.' Stephen Daisley, *The Spectator*

'Lyra's writing was confident and stylish. She had a voice that rang true . . . Lyra did not die for the cause of Irish freedom. Lyra was Irish freedom.' Susan McKay, *New Yorker*

'Everything Lyra did was informed by love for her region, for her community and for human rights . . . She hoped so much for Northern Ireland, but she herself was that hope.' Sarah Kay, *Independent*

'Even in the early stages of her career, McKee forged a voice brimming with empathy and integrity . . . McKee treats the nebulous political and social constraints, the multifaceted identities of the country and the individuals at its stormy heart with care and compassion. She shows an acute awareness of the horrors and violence her generation was spared from, while navigating their own stifling world . . . The brevity of this collection, quietly framed by the knowledge that she too was to be a victim of the unresolved trauma she so valiantly explored, inspires an ache deep in any reader. In this anthology we see a body of work by a writer who, while accomplished, was at the beginning of her burgeoning career.' Anna Cafolla, *Prospect*

'Unbearably poignant . . . [In *Lost, Found, Remembered*] we can see something of the bright curiosity and fierce compassion of a courageous voice whose time was cut cruelly, scandalously short.' Dan Brotzel, *Irish News*

LYRA McKEE

Lost, Found,
Remembered

faber

First published in 2020
by Faber & Faber Ltd
Bloomsbury House
74–77 Great Russell Street
London WC1B 3DA

This paperback edition published in 2021

Typeset by Ian Bahrami
Printed in the UK by CPI Group (UK) Ltd, Croydon, CRO 4YY

Permissions acknowledgements appear on pp. 183–4

A CIP record for this book
is available from the British Library

ISBN 978–0–571–35145–9

FSC
www.fsc.org
MIX
Paper from
responsible sources
FSC® C020471

2 4 6 8 10 9 7 5 3 1

Contents

REMEMBERED

They say that for years Belfast was backwards
and it's great now to see some progress.
So I guess we can look forward to taking boxes
from the earth. I guess that ambulances
will leave the dying back amidst the rubble
to be explosively healed. Given time,
one hundred thousand particles of glass
will create impossible patterns in the air
before coalescing into the clarity
of a window. Through which, a reassembled head
will look out and admire the shy young man
taking his bomb from the building and driving
    home.

'Progress', Alan Gillus

Editor's Note

As a writer Lyra McKee was drawn to subjects that are usually met with silence. She wrote about growing up gay in Northern Ireland, the epidemic of suicide among her generation in Belfast, and in her book for Faber, *The Lost Boys*, she was investigating the unsolved disappearances of children during the Troubles. She could always see the imprint of the Troubles in the graves freshly dug for those too young to fully remember the conflict, and it is heartbreaking that a continuation of that violence cut short her life. Lyra McKee asked the right questions and reported on the things that matter.

In publishing this posthumous book, our intention is to commemorate her writing and magnify her voice. The book is curated into three sections: unpublished work in 'Lost', pieces that may be less familiar to the reader in 'Found', and the pieces that cemented her reputation as one of her generation's most formidable journalists in 'Remembered'. This book is both a celebration of her talent and a reminder of what we have lost.

LOST

In My Own Words

I grew up in a 'conflict hotspot' in North Belfast, off a road known as Murder Mile because of the number of people who were killed on it during the Troubles. The Cliftonville Road – where I was born and reared – is said to have had more casualties per square foot during the war than any other part of the country. I've written extensively about the conflict because I know it so intimately. I witnessed its last years, as armed campaigns died and gave way to an uneasy tension we natives of Northern Ireland have named 'peace', and I lived with its legacy, watching friends and family members cope with the trauma of what they could not forget.

I dropped out of university aged nineteen. In 2006, I won the 'Sky News Young Journalist of the Year' for a story looking at rising suicide rates in my native North Belfast. I've been published in the *Atlantic*, *BuzzFeed News*, *Mosaic Science*, the *Independent*, and many other newspapers and magazines. In 2016, *Forbes* named me one of their 30 Under 30 best journalists in Europe. I have delivered newsroom training to journalists at newspapers including

Extracted from The Lost Boys' *author biography*

the *Daily Telegraph* and the *Sunday Times*. I have also worked for the Thomson Reuters Foundation, mentoring and overseeing investigations into financial corruption by Africa-based journalists.

I have spoken at events all over the world, including Techraking, a conference jointly organised by Google and the California Center for Investigative Reporting (CIR), journalism.co.uk's News Rewired event in London, the International Journalism Festival in Perugia, Italy, and TEDxStormont in Belfast. In 2014, 'Letter to My Fourteen-Year-Old Self', a story describing my experience of growing up as a gay person in Northern Ireland, went viral. It was later developed into the short film *Letter*, produced by Belfast-based production company Stay Beautiful films. It has since been screened at a US film festival.

I know very well how the Troubles masked other crimes; how women, children and vulnerable people were harmed because child abusers and killers and men who beat their wives don't stop doing what they do because there's a war on. In fact, they carry on because they can – because a police force and judicial system distracted by a war tend to overlook 'ordinary' criminals. And sometimes, they carry on because the war has turned them into a 'protected species' – like an IRA or UVF member who raped women but was too valuable to the organisation to be punished and who was secretly feeding information to the security services and was therefore too valuable an asset to them, too. Lots of awful things are done in the name of winning wars, but they are eventually reckoned with when the conflict ends and the families of the dead speak up about their loved ones.

Time is running out
Day is reigning longer than night
I used to take refuge in the stars
Each one marking an hour of time
Six and a half, a snatched moment here and there
To confess a truth, hidden, like pink
Blossoms, in white Dalmatian snow

Now the stars' brightness
Cannot be seen amid the sun's brightness
And I must tell all, and hear the truth
Before the stars no longer mark
A passage of time that I can see during waking
    hours
Before I must be on my way
Confess these truths
Love, in its own language, means
Seize the day

This poem is taken from a collection Lyra wrote when she was thirteen entitled Changing with the Seasons.

Awaiting the Snowflakes

I had that dream
During the prelude season to autumn
She told me grave, bitter news.
The doctors may as well have shattered my heart
With one of their fancy surgical knives.
Our dreams, not only my vital organs
Were cut into tiny slivers.
A new house in the spring awaited
She only had till Christmas.

Away from the harsh realities of fantasy
I walked along the shore.
The dark, choppy waters
Mirroring my thoughts.
Thoughts residing at God's mercy
Where I fervently prayed
For anything but her missing presence.
She was silent
Knowing not to bother me
Not knowing why.

My prayers were answered
Yet at the expense of someone else
Harbouring only a few weeks to live, I heard,
'A pity she didn't have till Christmas':
The snowflakes had yet to fall.

The following pieces are all excerpted from the book Lyra was working on at the time of her death: The Lost Boys. *They have not been published previously.*

They call my generation the 'Ceasefire Babies', though I've always hated that name. I hated the mocking tone in which it was usually said, as if growing up in the nineties in Belfast was a stroll. There were still soldiers on the street when I was a kid. I remember them – in uniforms and maroon berets, at checkpoints, on pavements, crouching down on one knee, as if ducking out of sight of an enemy the surrounding civilians couldn't see. I remember walking past one with my sister, then aged about sixteen, after she had picked me up from school. 'Do they wear hats on their heads to stop them from getting cold?' I'd asked, or something inane to that effect. 'Yes,' she'd replied, smiling, and the pale-skinned recruit I'd gestured to had smiled as well. Blond hair peeked out from underneath his cap. He looked barely older than her, perhaps eighteen. That was around the time I learned that the toy gun I used for games of Cowboys and Indians could not be brought outside, in case a passing patrol saw it and mistook it for a real one. It didn't matter that it was silver with an orange trumpet-top on the end of the barrel; you couldn't take any chances.

It had happened, my mother assured me, to a little boy, on the same street where I'd seen the teen soldier. I was never sure if this was truth or urban legend, but the only time I took the gun outside, to the backyard – which was surrounded by a ten-foot concrete wall – I'd had the arse smacked off me. The helicopters were out; what if they'd seen it with their cameras, my mother said, and thought it was real? The scenario seemed unlikely to me: that a helicopter, thousands of feet up in the air, would spot a kid playing with a toy and send a patrol to our house. But my mother wasn't taking any chances.

*

Northern Ireland had a way of burying uncomfortable truths, just like it buried its dead. Grief operated according to a strict hierarchy here back then. If your loved one had been killed in the Troubles, you were guaranteed the attention of local politicians. Conflict victims were a unique form of political currency, bartered by each side. Victims of the Irish Republican Army (IRA) would regularly be rolled out by the Unionists; Army and police victims, by the Republicans. Those whose loved ones had been involved with the paramilitaries received less sympathy, particularly if they were Protestants, but at some point, they would see their loved one's name mentioned in the paper. They wouldn't be allowed to forget what had happened. Journalists wanted to talk to them, even if they didn't want to talk back.

*

Things have changed since the ceasefire. I think it's possible, for the first time – for someone of my generation – to write about the conflict from a historical perspective. And yet, like so much of the recent past, it's haunting, too. It's all still there, just underneath the surface of things. A friend of mine, the documentary maker Ali Millar, has an office in South Belfast, at the edge of a district which was battered during the Troubles. At the corner of the street, a mural on the side of a house commemorates William of Orange, who'd landed in the country three centuries before. Every July, local residents in the mostly Protestant area celebrate him with a day of marching, a country-wide event which has been branded 'Orangefest' by the tourism board, in an attempt to make it more PR-friendly to visitors. Natives, though, called it the Twelfth. In rural parts, it is centred around innocent family activities, but in the city

– in the form that I knew it – it could often descend into drunken riots and fights with the neighbouring Catholic community or the police.

What was most interesting about the mural, though, was what it had replaced. It had been carefully painted over the top of another, less tourist-friendly image, this one of a man in a balaclava holding a semi-automatic rifle, with the words 'YOU ARE NOW ENTERING LOYALIST SANDY ROW HEARTLAND OF SOUTH BELFAST ULSTER FREEDOM FIGHTERS' emblazoned in bold, black type, framed by icons of red fists. One man's freedom fighter was another man's terrorist, and to many of the Protestant population and their Catholic neighbours, the freedom fighters who had been commemorated in this memorial were just that – terrorists. The area was a thirty-second walk from the Great Victoria Street station, the terminus point for visitors arriving from the local airports or Dublin by bus.

Sometimes, you'd walk by and see them – tourists with cameras, hovering in front of William's painting, seemingly oblivious to what had been on the wall before it. Throughout the city, murals dedicated to the terror groups who'd once ruled the districts were slowly being erased. It was a whitewashing of the past and it was happening because we were desperate for the world to know us for any reason other than war. Maybe we were trying to erase our own memories, hoping for a collective amnesia by blotting out reminders of what had happened. But all you had to do was scratch the paint and you'd find the city's past, like a ghost that refused to depart for the other world.

*

A History of the Troubles Accordin' to a Ceasefire Baby

When the conflict ended in Northern Ireland, the fight turned from guns to history books. 'Ended' was a euphemism, I thought, because it never truly seemed to end, so much as it changed shape, with the gunmen and those in charge of them concluding that violence was not the best way to win a war. Republicans – represented mainly by Sinn Fein, the political wing of the Provisionals, and mainly emanating from the Catholic community – maintained that the British had no right to be in Northern Ireland. The Unionists – represented by numerous warring factions but mainly the Democratic Unionist Party (DUP) – maintained that they did. Yet the 'constitutional question' – over whether the Northern six counties should be reunited with the Southern twenty-six counties or remain in Britain's clasp – was not what absorbed the attention of former combatants and their supporters. Whereas before they killed those they perceived to be their enemy – combatants on the other side, civilians, police officers, priests, soldiers, children – now, they struggled with them for control of the narrative and how history would come to view them all. The debates were forever being recycled on radio and television talk shows:

'That murder was justified, he was working for the police!'

'The Royal Ulster Constabulary were a fantastic police force being gunned down by terrorists.'

'Excuse me, the IRA were not terrorists, they were freedom fighters, and they would never have had to pick up a gun if British soldiers hadn't come on to the streets and started killing civilians!'

'The British soldiers were there protecting us, they would never have had to come in if the IRA wasn't bombing innocents!'

'The IRA were freedom fighters!'

'No, they weren't, the Loyalist groups like the UVF were freedom fighters, protecting us from the IRA—'

'They were terrorists!'

'The RUC were terrorists! They were colluding with the Loyalists!'

'That's a slur on our police officers.'

'You just can't admit to what your side did! Killing innocents!'

It was endless. Between 1969 and 1998, 3,700 men, women and children had been slaughtered in bombings, shootings and more. Their killers ranged from Provisional IRA members to members of the Loyalist terror groups – the Ulster Volunteer Force (UVF), Ulster Defence Association (UDA), Ulster Freedom Fighters (UFF) – British soldiers and corrupt police officers. Whether you justified or condemned each murder sometimes depended on which one, the victim or the perpetrator, came from your community. If the murderer was one of your own, then the more hardline members of the Tribe – because that's what we were, a group thrown together by virtue of the altar we worshipped at on Sundays – expected you to lay out the reasons as to why murder was sometimes permissible. I was born into the Catholic faith, four years before the Provisional IRA announced a ceasefire and eight years before the signing of the peace accord, the Good Friday Agreement. This meant I was expected to condemn all murders of innocent Catholics and IRA/Republican volunteers, while approving the murders of 'legitimate targets' ranging

17

from police officers to British soldiers and any civilian or volunteer who turned 'tout' and passed information on to the security services. As for collateral damage, the poor Prods and Catholics who accidentally wandered into the path of a bomb, their deaths were regrettable but not so much that they besmirched the cause or the movement or the volunteer who'd deposited the device on a crowded street on a busy afternoon. To betray the Tribe and not stick to the script was almost as bad as being a tout. Any mention of casualties from the other side – of the children who'd died in IRA bombs or who'd witnessed their fathers being shot dead in their own living room – was never to be acknowledged, only met with a reminder of the lives lost in Loyalist bombings and shootings. Such defences had a name: 'Whataboutery'.

The Other Tribe lived by the same rules. The rules were not unique to us. We were all governed by these unspoken and unwritten laws. And yet the strange thing was, it was not always the ex-prisoners, those who'd fought for the IRA and UVF and UDA and all the other factions, who expected you to uphold the rituals and defend what they'd done. While each terror group had ideological aims – to gain a United Ireland (the IRA) or protect British rule (the UVF et al.) – the youths who'd joined them had generally done so for what had seemed like good reasons at the time. Often, it was a death in the family that triggered their decision to sign up: a cousin who'd had his head blown off as he walked the half mile from the pub to his home, or a brother killed when he answered a knock on the front door to a gunman waiting outside. Death had been so random during the Troubles and could visit your door at any moment. I didn't agree with what they had done, but it was easy to make such moral proclamations while living in a time of peace. I'd only seen the tail end of the war, and that had been bad enough. Could I have lived through the worst of it and held on to my morals? When you were surrounded by people with guns and you didn't know if they were coming for you next, did having access to a gun yourself give you a false sense of power? Did it make you feel as if you'd reduced the odds of Death coming for your family? War was as complicated as it was ugly, and the person you were when you lived through it was probably different to the person who emerged after. Many of those calling in to the morning radio talk shows, arguing for the narrative which cast their side in the best light, hadn't spent twenty years in a 4 × 4-foot cell musing on these matters. The ex-prisoners had, and, among the ones I knew at least, joy and justification over their past deeds were in short supply. Most were stuck somewhere between remorse and empathy for their younger selves.

When it came to ex-prisoners, certain sections of society and the media had a tendency to cast them as evil, as servants of Satan himself who were far beyond the redemption of any God or religion. I understood that. I couldn't stand in front of a woman who'd watched her husband be gunned down, in front of their children, perhaps in their own living room, and tell her that the men who'd done it were more complex than evil and more human than her grief would allow her to believe. I hadn't lost anyone. Yet still I didn't see the ex-prisoners as being beyond redemption. I'd seen evil amongst their number. I'd also seen men and women struggling to reconcile their present selves to what their past selves had done. Many were dying by the bottle or by suicide. They couldn't live with themselves. Why they wanted to hasten a meeting with their maker, I didn't know. Many of them seemed to have stopped believing in God a long time ago, so maybe they believed death was an escape into nothingness. I had friends who'd been in the IRA during the Troubles and a dear friend who'd been a cop in the RUC, trying to put as many of the former away behind bars as he possibly could, as well as their counterparts in the Loyalist groups.

The irony was that all of them, enemies who'd fought on opposing sides or sides which sometimes worked together but were more often apart, were facing the same struggles in peacetime. They all seemed to loathe sleep because sleep brought nightmares. They all woke up screaming in the middle of the night.

Many people have grown to dislike the use of the word 'war' to describe what happened here. The term 'the conflict' became a more acceptable alternative, even if it made a thirty-year battle sound like a lovers' tiff. It's got the ring of a euphemism, the kind one might use to refer to a shameful family secret during a reunion lunch. Part of the argument was that the victims felt calling it 'war' gave legitimacy to terrorist groups and their volunteers, allowed them to view themselves as soldiers – either in the cause of saving Ireland from British rule, or of saving it from those who wanted to save it from British rule.

But we were to be the generation to avoid all that. We were to reap the spoils and prosperity that supposedly came with peace. In the end, we did get the peace – or something close to it – and those who'd caused carnage in the decades before got the money. Whether they'd abandoned arms (as the Provisionals did) or retained them (like the Loyalists), they'd managed to make a ton of paper. We got to live with the outcome of their choices. But before I tell you about how my generation got fucked over, I should probably talk a little about how the war started in the first place. You probably know this story, or parts of it, but let me tell it to you in my own words, because the answer to the question depends on who you ask, and how far back you want to go; and so my own take matters.

*

Northern Ireland was created in 1921 after the southern twenty-six counties broke away from British rule, following the Easter Rising – a rebellion – five years before. The north of the country had a solid Protestant population who considered themselves British subjects and wanted to retain the link with the UK. So the rebels got their twenty-six counties, which would eventually become known as the Republic of Ireland, and the UK got to keep the remaining six. This would have been a perfectly satisfactory solution were it not for the sizable minority of Catholics left stranded there on the wrong side of the new border.

The Catholic civilians didn't protest much. They'd been all but abandoned by the rebel leaders in the South, so they might have settled down and integrated well with the majority. They were native-born, after all, and British rule was the only rule they'd ever known. But in their newly created country, they were abandoned by London and left to face bouts of violence and discrimination. Protestants received preferential treatment in the form of housing and jobs, a status quo actively encouraged by the Unionist politicians of the time. The likes of the Harland and Wolff shipyard, which sat at the edge of East Belfast and built the *Titanic*, employed Protestants almost exclusively.

My friends and I would argue about this all the time.

'I don't remember my grandparents having any money. They lived in poverty with an outside toilet.' We were in a grimy Wetherspoon's near the edge of the student district in South Belfast, sandwiched between the city centre and the road that led to the William of Orange mural. Most of its clientele were working-class Prods. With the bus station and Queen's University nearby, it drew in its fair share of tourists and students, too. Three decades before, whatever establishment it had been then, it wouldn't have been safe for me to be there, drinking among a bunch of tattooed Loyalists, especially with such an obviously Gaelic name: 'Leer-rah'. The pronunciation would give me away instantly. In fact, it still wouldn't have been safe for me to go into a pub in a Loyalist stronghold. This place, though, was a geographical no-man's-land that anyone could lay claim to, and the Prods, tourists, students and

I drank together amiably enough, lured in by the promise of cheap food and booze. I'd been visiting Spoons on and off for ten years, first as a student and then into adulthood and the world of work; while I was definitely better off than I had been, journalism did not a luxurious lifestyle fund. Besides, it was a neutral venue for meeting Will. Like mine, his name gave him away – William was usually a name reserved for Prods. We could have met near my place; the area I lived in was becoming slowly gentrified, with a mix of Protestants and Catholics moving in, but the local pubs still retained their more hardened clientele – people who'd supported the IRA and would have bristled had they thought there was a Loyalist in their midst. The ex-prisoners themselves, those who'd actually been in the organisation or one of its splinter groups, were much more relaxed; they'd probably have bought him a pint. That could have been said of ex-prisoners in general; it was always the armchair commandos who were the rowdiest. Will was from the east of the city, but I felt too nervous to venture into one of the working men's pubs there. So, Spoons it was, barely a two-minute walk from the city centre and a halfway point between us. 'How were your grandparents any worse off than mine?' We'd had this argument before – always in Spoons.

'Because yours were given jobs,' I said. 'And housing. Look at what happened in Caledon.'

Caledon was a tiny village in County Tyrone, near the border with the Republic of Ireland. There, in 1967, a family called the Gildernews had decided to squat in a house, in protest at discrimination against Catholics. The house had been granted by the local council to a single nineteen-year-old Protestant woman who happened to be the secretary for a Unionist politician. The Gildernews' protest led to the organisation of civil rights marches throughout the province. It became a movement, drawing inspiration from the campaign across the water in the US. It was one of many signs of discontent before the Troubles began.

I reminded him about 'one man, one vote', too. Under Unionist rule in the 1950s and 1960s, only ratepayers and their spouses could vote in elections – owning or renting multiple properties entitled you to multiple votes. Since Unionists fared better in terms of jobs and housing, these rules favoured them.

'That was bad for my grandparents as well as yours!' he replied. 'They didn't own more than one house.'

I hadn't considered that. Catholics in 1960s Northern Ireland had had legions of grievances. They'd since been remedied but, still, that sense of resentment had been passed down through the generations. We – their descendants – were no longer out protesting. Instead, we sat in pubs with our Protestant friends and bitched at each other about the things their 'side' had done to ours, and vice versa. It was nasty but kind of irresistible, like picking at a scab. We should have been worrying about the future, not the past. The prospect of a harder border between the North and the South, as a result of Brexit, was looming like the shadow of a TV villain. The peace we'd enjoyed for twenty years was fragile at best. Even after the signing of the Good Friday Agreement in 1998, it had taken some time for the interface areas – where Protestants and Catholics lived on either side of a dividing road – to feel less like a war zone. The old tensions would return every July, when the Orange Order marched down the Crumlin Road, much to the chagrin of residents in Republican Ardoyne. Peace was an acquaintance rather than a friend. But we were alive and more likely to die by our own hands than somebody else's. I didn't know which was worse, but nor did I want to go back to those days and find out.

Even this, though – sitting in a pub, arguing with a friend from the other side of the peace wall – was an incredibly middle-class thing to do. Neither of us were born middle-class; we grew into it. We'd both grown up in what were euphemistically called 'deprived' areas. Deprived or disadvantaged were just polite ways of saying shithole. If you lived in one of those areas and never managed to escape, it was unlikely you had friends from the other side to test your beliefs against. In recent years, youths from Ardoyne, a large Catholic area, and the nearby Protestant enclave of the Shankill had met on cross-community trips and befriended each other. They would travel back and forth on visits. It was welcome progress, but the two communities were still fundamentally segregated – living in separate areas, going to separate schools. At a grassroots level, community workers weaved miracles and brought them together. At a political level, though, there was a lack of will to do that. For the bigger parties, playing on tribal fears was still the go-to strategy for getting voters to turn up at the polling station.

So how did the conflict begin? The point is this: if you asked someone from Will's community how the war started, they would blame the IRA. The IRA had wanted a United Ireland, they'd argue, and they were determined to get it at any cost. They would bomb, kill and maim if they had to – and they'd done so, with gusto. The Unionist community only had the police and the Army to protect them. And, some would add, terror groups like the UVF and UDA.

If, on the other hand, you asked someone from the community I was born into, you'd get a similar answer but with the roles reversed. In that version, the IRA were the protectors of the Catholic population, guarding them from all manner of evils: a mostly Protestant police force with corrupt officers; British soldiers who shot civilians on sight and rounded up young men, interning them without trial; Loyalist gunmen who roamed Catholic areas, often at night, and picked victims at random.

Which side was telling the truth? The most honest answer was that paramilitaries had killed both innocent Catholics and innocent Protestants.

The weirdest thing, though, was this: if you spoke to an IRA-supporting Republican – someone who wanted a United Ireland – they would list every injustice visited on Catholics by the Army, the police, the Loyalists and the British state. They would never mention that more Catholics had been killed by the IRA than by all those other factions put together.

UVF/UDA-supporting Unionists (known as Loyalists) would give a similar – but, again, inverted – answer. They would list every Republican atrocity, murder and injustice, but the names of innocent Catholics who'd been slaughtered – and, in some cases, those of Protestants – would never pass their lips.

As for me, I would say that the Troubles began partly because the IRA spotted an opportunity. In the 1940s and 1950s, their armed campaigns had failed, mostly due to a lack of support from the Catholic population. By 1969, though, tensions were spilling over, with Catholics being burned out of their homes by Loyalist mobs. They heard rumours of the same mobs being assisted by the police, who were mostly Protestants themselves. The community was developing a kind of Stockholm relationship with the Provos – too afraid to stand up to them but depending on them for protection, too. And by 1972, the Parachute Regiment of the British Army had killed over two dozen innocent civilians in Belfast and Derry, in the Ballymurphy Massacre and Bloody Sunday. This had only reinforced the Catholics' fears and made them more dependent on the IRA. Decades later, Sinn Fein would claim the Provisionals' campaign had been about securing equal rights. But that was a lie. In '69, I reckoned, some of their leaders probably fancied themselves to be like the 1916 rebels and believed they could score a coup, forcing the Brits to the negotiating table. Similarly, the leaders of the terror groups emerging from the Protestant community thought of themselves as the defenders of the province. No one – not the Brits, not the Loyalists and not the IRA – expected the Troubles to last thirty years.

The motivations of the foot soldiers who joined the groups, though, were often simpler than any of this suggests. I'd go to interview fifty-something ex-prisoners, covered in tattoos but ultimately softened by decades of three meals a day and lights out at 8 p.m., and leave with a different image: of the frightened sixteen-year-old they'd once been. When you were a working-class kid with no money and no prospects and feared people more violent than you, nothing made you feel as powerful as a weapon in your fist.

That seemed to be how the IRA and the UDA and all the other groups sucked recruits in: fear. As the war dragged on, it became about other things. Money. Sex. Greed. Power. Being senior in one of these groups came with status. Women threw themselves at you. There was the risk of prison, but if you avoided that, there was more money than you could imagine – particularly if you operated near the top of the organisation. An ex-Special Branch officer once told me how, in 1985, he'd observed a UDA brigadier and Provo leaders in a bar in Belfast city centre – the Capstan in Ann Street. They were negotiating the carve-up of building sites. Back then, everyone from builders to shopkeepers had to pay 'protection money' to whatever group was running the area. If they didn't pay it, they couldn't work there. It still happens now, even in peacetime. The lower Newtownards Road, a Protestant area, was pocked with shuttered windows, the remnants of small businesses that couldn't afford the regular payout to the Loyalists.

So it wasn't just ideology; it never is. War was a business, and nothing proved it like collaborating with the enemy to make money. Of course, the backroom deals of the officer class wouldn't have been known to the average volunteer. Later, some of those who'd been ground-level troops in the IRA would speak out, feeling like the years they'd spent in prison had all been for nothing. They viewed the peace deal as a betrayal. What had been the purpose of it all, if the end point was going to be an armistice? Some met with their counterparts in the UVF and compared notes, trying to figure out who or what or how they'd been fucked over. Had it been the plan all along – to sell out? With hindsight, some of them believed it had.

*

The story of how my generation got fucked over was a different one. We didn't sign up to a war and get sold out by a surrender. Instead, politicians, hoping to sell the peace deal to our parents, made three promises.

The first promise, they barely delivered on: peace. Loyalist paramilitaries stopped terrorising Catholic neighbourhoods; instead, they terrorised their own. The Provisional IRA and various Republican splinter groups faded away, but in their place new groups grew, with names like 'the New IRA'. Like the Loyalists, they instilled fear in poor areas like Ardoyne, which were only beginning to get over the past three decades. In the background, Unionist and Republican or Nationalist politicians continued to bicker, reopening old wounds and appealing to the sectarian fears of their voters at every election. It wasn't the peace promised, just an absence of all-out civil war. Shootings still happened, but it was no longer each side against the other; the paramilitaries were now aiming their guns inwards, towards their own communities.

The second promise was prosperity. Peace, we were assured, would bring a thriving new economy. It never appeared. It didn't matter what qualifications you had, the most plentiful work was to be found in call centres, answering or making calls for a minimum wage. They were egalitarian shitholes; middle-class kids with PhDs mixed with kids with no GCSEs, and they all earned the same for doing the same grunt work. If you were lucky, the job didn't come with timed toilet breaks. In the end, most graduates ended up leaving. People who'd been searching for jobs for two years in Northern Ireland would find one within eight weeks in London. But it was like escaping from one trap only to walk into another; London offered jobs but it didn't offer a life. Most people I knew out there were just scraping by, paying £650 a month for a bedroom in a grotty apartment. Eventually, they'd figure out you couldn't buy a house for £100K in London the way you could in Belfast and would either return, settling for what work they could find and swapping career dreams for family life, or head further afield.

The third promise the politicians made and broke was the one that hurt the most. It was felt mostly in the areas that had already been ravaged, the ones where the gunmen continued to roam. Your children, they'd told our parents, will be safe now. With the peace deal, the days of young people disappearing and dying young would be gone.

Yet this turned out to be a lie, too.

*

The shop was stacked wall-to-wall with second-hand washing machines. The counter where a shop till would normally be was a slab from a kitchen tabletop placed over a piece of wood. The decor was basic, simple, but the shop's existence in itself was an achievement.

Shaun was a working-class boy. We'd grown up in the same streets, a five-minute walk from the shop. It had once been a middle-class area, a collection of tree-lined avenues and narrow terraced houses which could still fit four bedrooms inside because they stretched out over three to four flights of stairs. That was before we were born, long enough ago to become history remembered only by the elderly neighbours. Then the Troubles had started, the posh people fled, and now the houses were occupied by everyone from criminals to those too sick to work to those too lazy to. These were not the working classes but the benefits classes. For them, the dole office was not a brief stepping stone after redundancy but a permanent fixture on the calendar – Monday morning, 9 a.m. usually. In the social pecking order, Shaun's standing had been slightly higher than the rest of us because his mother owned houses, but he still had to live among us and deal with the torture that came with living in a place without hope. When people, especially young men, had no hope, all incentives not to wreck the place were gone, and wreck it they did. The area continued to be a battlefield long after the conflict had technically ended, devouring itself from within.

Shaun had escaped. He was a grafter. Always had been. Even back when he was a teenager, drifting through the area on his skateboard, he displayed something unique. One day, a skateshop in the city centre was making a film about local skaters and had wanted him to jump down a set of steps, flipping the board mid-air as he went. He'd screwed it up the first time. And the second. Third. Fourth. Finally, on the fifth attempt – so local lore had it – he'd nailed the move and landed, intact, at the bottom of the steps. His willingness to keep trying until he did it, while risking bone fractures or worse, had become legendary amongst the group of local outcasts who also carried boards or wore skates.

The preferred uniform of the area was tracksuit bottoms paired with a hoody. Deviating away from it meant attracting attention, and attention was never good here, only bad. Somehow, though, Shaun had managed to straddle both worlds, drinking with the hoods, then befriending the minority of nerds and skaters who skulked around the streets trying to see round corners, hoping not to be noticed. Apart from the cops, who I once saw roll down their windows and call out taunts about his size, no one had a bad word to say about Shaun. Across the road was the Waterworks. It was a North Belfast landmark, iconic both because of its size and the fact that the Germans had bombed it in the Second World War, yet here it still stood. It was a park that stretched from a dirty, man-made, polluted pond on the lower ground up a hill to a lake with silky blue waters that lapped a stone shore. It was the bane of Shaun's life. Drug dealers would hang around its perimeter, flogging their wares in full view of the busy main road and passing police cars. It would send him hurtling into a rage. One day, he'd hopped on his motorbike – it was a beast of a machine and he was barely five foot four, but he was athletic enough to command it – and chased them up the road. They were bad for business, but I had a feeling his anger had little to do with money. When he was around sixteen, he'd walked into a derelict house that had stood near the corner of Manor Street, a regular haunt for teens in the district because of the corner shop, which sold cigarettes in singles. He'd begun climbing the stairs.

Why had he been there? What had he been looking for? It wasn't clear, but Shaun's intuition was usually solid and I imagined it was a nagging, that something's-not-right feeling anyone who'd grown up with the violence of the streets seemed to possess. At the top of the stairs, he'd wandered into a room. There, suspended from the rafters by a piece of rope, had been the body of his best friend. He'd cut the boy down, presumably begun making the phone calls that needed to be made. Fifteen years later, he could still picture the scene in his head, describe what had happened that night as if it was a movie he'd just seen in the cinema. Many had died the same way since, and we'd known them or known of them. The incident hadn't ruined his life, but when he saw dealers, the kind of people who did ruin the lives of the young, kids who'd been the same age as his best friend when he'd died or younger, he flew into a rage, the kind of rage where you'd do something reckless like take off in pursuit of a group of criminals because you know the cops had no interest in arresting them.

It was what I loved about Shaun. He cared.

There was a reason I went searching for the body that day. I can't say it was solely because I wanted to find him. The other volunteers out searching on the mountain were doing so in hope, believing that maybe the boy had fallen or tripped and hurt his leg and just couldn't make his way home. But I knew he was dead. I'd seen the same story play out before and it always concluded with headlines that said: 'Body found in hunt for missing lad'. We were looking for a corpse and I was torn between wanting to find it and not wanting to. Finding it would mean being the person who dashed hopes that he was still alive. The thought of making that phone call made an icy feeling grow in my stomach.

I referred to him as 'the boy' even though he was a man. He was old enough to smoke, vote and drink but too young to die. The week he went missing came after a season of storms. They had felled trees and power lines, turned the mountain slopes into slush and the ocean treacherous. It was a bad time to go missing, if you had any hope of being found, and a bad time to be out looking for a body.

The boy probably didn't want to be found. It was all but a certainty that he had committed suicide somewhere on the slopes above. The volunteers, I believed, knew it too, even though they were lying to themselves because no one wanted to give up hope until they had to.

When the call went out on social media – 'Appeal: Man, young, missing, last seen—' – the search, always, would begin with mountains and parks and rivers. Tree branches would be scanned by volunteers with binoculars, water by divers with specialist equipment. In the first twenty-four hours, there was a chance you could reach the missing lad – it was always a lad – before he made it to a bridge or a peak or a lonely clearing in the woods. By forty-eight hours, the more experienced searchers would be mentally preparing themselves to find a corpse.

Maybe he had wanted to deny his family that sight, believing that not knowing his fate was better than knowing. It seemed logical – the reason so many of them disappeared into the water or the woods. We'd all seen the havoc a dead body could wreak. You didn't have to actually have seen one to know. As surely as people from the Welsh valleys knew coal miners or Scots knew the taste of haggis, Northern Irish youths knew someone who'd been murdered. It was there in nearly every family, a ghost in the background somewhere. Sometimes, it was an aunt or an uncle or a father or grandmother. Other times, the connection was looser – your da's best friend, forever seventeen, shot in the head as he walked to the first job he'd ever had. It was all around us.

Some were consumed by the memories and loaded their children with them, like bags on to a mule. Others buried them. But grief was persistent. It hung thick over its victims. It manifested itself in night terrors and alcoholism and PTSD and an inability to forget. They called us, the young, the Ceasefire Babies because we were born either around or after the time of the Provisional IRA ceasefire, in the last four years of the Troubles before it 'ended'. We, the elders believed, would never see or know war the way they had. But we did. We just saw it through their eyes.

So I understood the boy's reasoning, why he'd taken to the hills to die. It probably seemed like the lesser evil – to leave loved ones without a body, to let them think – in the absence of evidence – that you'd just had enough and had decided to escape. Others had done it throughout the conflict – just vanished into thin air, leaving their family to wonder whether they were alive or dead.

As mountains went, Cave Hill was no Everest. It felt wrong to even call it a mountain. It stood at seven hundred feet, throwing the northern edges of the city into shadow. Along its peak ran rough cliff-like walls of volcanic rock, steep vertical drops which offered certain death if leaped from. At its foot, a path that veered from gravel to muck and back again could take you straight to the top, with moderate difficulty. It was – should have been – an easy climb, if you just followed it up from the foot of the mountain. We didn't. It seemed unlikely that the body would be there, on the well-travelled route.

The decision to join the hunt was made the night before.

'I wanna help out with the search,' Stuart had said. Stuart, not much taller than I was at five foot six, was nonetheless a man built for mountains: sturdy, with a little bit of loose muscle hanging over an otherwise slim frame. He had a large, heavy mop of silvery grey hair, which contrasted heavily with a boyish, stubble-flecked face. A scriptwriter, he liked to spend his time in between drafts and takes by hiking large peaks, for reasons I couldn't quite fathom.

'Up the mountain?'

'Aye,' he replied. 'There's a route the volunteers haven't looked, I don't think. There's a few places I'd like to check out, in the more remote parts.' He took a bite of his burrito. After a few pints in the local Wetherspoon's, we'd migrated to a Mexican chain food eatery that served white people versions of what Mexican food actually was. For £7 a meal, though, it was tasty, and given that scriptwriters and journalists were in the same wage bracket – as in, if you were lucky, you made enough money to pay rent but not enough to eat out anywhere but a chain restaurant – it suited both of us.

'Where you gonna look exactly?'

'I don't know,' he said. He paused for a second. 'I've just got a hunch there's a few places they haven't checked.'

The son of a Church of Ireland preacher, Stuart had grown up in a small town called Monaghan in the Republic of Ireland before eventually settling in North Belfast as a teenager. He'd fallen in love with that corner of the city in a way that only someone who'd spent time apart from it could, looking at it with a fondness tinged by absence. He'd come back as it was changing, with New York-style loft apartments and delis and fish shops which no longer served chips but 'gourmet' meals. It had taken a decade for the North to feel the effects of gentrification. Here, the residents were the poorest in the country, never mind inside the city limits. Still, even as the shop fronts changed, with grease-stained interiors in cafes replaced by fine wood panelling and the latest in hipster decor, it was forever marked in my eyes as the same shithole I'd spent most of my life trying to climb out of. Maybe Stuart's Christian upbringing meant he could shake off bitterness easier than I could. I'd known too many who had died, who'd gone up Cave Hill not planning to return. Some had just fashioned a noose out of a leather belt and were found, hanging, from the door handle of their bedroom. I could count their names on my fingers until I ran out of hands and then trace each death, in some way, to the city and its history and a time when there was at least one murder every day. The city itself was like a noose and if you couldn't untangle yourself from it, it would choke you too.

'I'll go with you,' I said.

I didn't know the young lad but I knew the mountain. By all accounts, he was handsome, talented and well loved, judging by the seemingly hundreds who'd ascended the mountain looking for him. The morning he'd disappeared, he'd been seen by a neighbour, heading up the peaks for a walk – and no one had seen him come down.

*

'Are you prepared for the fact that we might find a dead body?'

It had been raining. The dirt track that led up to the back entrance of Cave Hill was slick with muck. The potholes dotting it had turned into puddles of brown water. Adjacent to my tiny Volkswagen Polo was a white Bentley, glistening amid the filth. Maybe its owner had hired help to clean it daily. The thought didn't seem far-fetched, judging by the house it sat outside. With a large brown gate fencing off intruders, it had a rectangular glass front, almost like a box, which surely made it hell to live in on a hot day. Yet hot days were few and far between in Northern Ireland. The owner probably had a second home elsewhere, in some sunnier climate. Besides, it was clear the house had been designed to an approved brief. It sat near the top of the hill, standing out from the dwellings perched below – magnificent redbricks themselves. They'd sell for at least £250K on the market. Some corners of the North – just a few – attracted the middle classes. They tended to congregate around the foot of the country estate that housed the mountain, despite the amount of underage drinking and drug taking and Lord knew what else that went on in it. This was where the doctors, the civil servants and the other citizens of the middle classes lived. They'd somehow emerged unscathed out of a failing economy. Unlike us, they had prospects.

'Yeah,' I replied. 'Maybe. Just about.' Silently, I said a prayer that there would be no dead bodies to be found, though I knew it was futile. If the boy was on the mountain, he was dead.

'This is kind of like *Stand by Me*,' Stuart said, shifting his backpack. 'You seen that movie? This is how their adventure starts. They go looking for a dead body.'

'I've read the book.' I'd read it only a few months before. It was a form of research. I didn't read it to learn how to search for a dead body but to get a sense of how I might feel when I eventually found one.

We got out of the car and began to walk. At the top of the path, close to the glass house, a bungalow sat in the corner, behind a row of hedges and a gate. It had probably once belonged to a farmer who'd tended to sheep on the hills above. Beside it, the gravel road continued through a broad gateway.

The official search had been organised via social networks. Volunteers had met at 10 a.m., two hours earlier. It was now 12 p.m. and we were only getting started.

'If he's come up here, he's come up here to die,' Stu said. We'd veered off the road, into an undergrowth of trees and fallen branches. For those in the north of the city, Cave Hill was becoming a bit like Aokigahara, the forest in Japan where lost souls went when they couldn't take any more. Bodies had been found here throughout the years – some having slipped and fallen, others having jumped. Yet this was the second search for a young man in as many months.

Fifteen years before, the suicides had started – or seemed to start – in Ardoyne, a formerly hardline Republican area in the city. It had started with one local kid. Six weeks later, thirteen of them would be dead, and parents were left wondering how so many young could die in a community of just a few thousand.

It had become contagious. One after another, they began to die – a thirteen-year-old here, a sixteen-year-old there. Some I only knew to see. Then the older folks started dying the same way.

It baffled families, journalists and politicians alike. Every 'outbreak' – four deaths or more within a five-mile radius – was treated with fresh horror, as if it was happening for the first time, even over a decade after it had first begun. Some politicians acted as if it wasn't obvious why people would grow up here and feel like life wasn't worth living. Did they deliberately turn their eyes from it?

Maybe it was the best way of sidestepping awkward questions at election time about why young people were still dying when the peace process had promised an end to all that. It was 2018, nearly twenty years to the day since the Good Friday Agreement was signed. It had been sold on the backs of the young, on the promise that the next two decades would be better for us than the previous thirty years had been for our parents and grandparents. Yet here we were, scattered across the mountain, searching for the dead. I knew we'd be back here eventually, looking for another body.

Maybe the politicians just lived a world apart from the people having to cut their children down from trees. The victims were disproportionately working-class – poor kids growing up in Shittown, Alabama, with no prospects and no hope of ever leaving. Belfast was a city you could fall in love with, but only if you were middle-class. It only revealed its best side to those with enough money to enjoy it – the new restaurants opening up, the hotels, the attractions. If you were poor, it had nothing to offer. The paramilitaries' targets had shifted; now, they almost exclusively killed members of their own communities, those who'd fallen short of the tribal laws they were expected to live by. If you didn't have the money to escape, to flee to London or the suburbs where the lawyers and doctors and civil servants lived, it was like the Troubles had never ended.

'I'm just going to check something here,' Stu said. He wandered off, disappearing beneath a tangle of leaves and branches and thorns, which appeared to have been decimated in the recent storms. A few feet away, a tiny stream bounced over brown stones. With the rain, the grass beneath my feet squelched, creating eerie sound effects in the silence. I glanced around. Stu was out of sight. I scanned the overgrowth in case someone had crept up and we hadn't heard them coming. It was paranoia, but I hated green spaces. The city's green belt was slowly evaporating, but during the Troubles, the paramilitaries had turned these areas into graveyards. Slightly further north, just beyond the city limits, there was a quiet road that led to the edges of the mountain's lower slopes. Some of the paramilitaries would use it to make their kill and then leave the body, phoning a tip in to the police using a code name. These were just the victims we knew of – the corpses they'd intended for the cops to find and the press to write about. I wondered how many times I'd walked over the top of a grave without knowing it.

I poked under some of the fallen branches, pulling them back. The greenery was so dense; it would be too easy to miss something – a grey shoe obscured by a tree trunk, or a glimpse of a pair of legs.

'Stu?'

'I'm here,' he called back. He reappeared a few seconds later. 'I just wanted to check down there, just in case.' He glanced across the stream. Beneath the cluster of trees, a clearing was visible. He walked towards it.

On either side of it, it looked as if someone had heaped a bunch of dead grass and weeds, forming what could have been a hobbit's house. Beyond, to the right, there was another mess of branches and leaves. He disappeared again through the overgrowth. I extended my foot, prodding the heap of grass and weeds. I was afraid they would fall apart and reveal something I didn't want to see.

Stu reappeared and walked towards a line of trees where the ground became noticeably steep. From here, the trees became even more dense. We began to climb.

Another ten or twenty feet upwards there were foot imprints embedded in the mud. Large, they looked like they probably belonged to a male.

'Well, someone's been here,' Stu said.

'Yeah, but he's been missing for days. With all this bad weather, would those tracks have lasted since then?'

'Hmm. Could have been a volunteer or someone out for a walk.'

'It's either a volunteer or it's him,' I said. 'I can't see somebody taking this route if they're just out for a walk, not in this weather; they'd know better. A volunteer, maybe, but I don't think they've covered this part.'

'I'm just thinking, if it was me,' he said, 'I'd be going this way. I'd be going off the beaten track. Somewhere you wouldn't find me.'

We kept climbing. It was another fifty feet up the slope before Stu realised his mistake.

'I thought there was a path up here,' he said. 'That was why I wanted to climb up through the trees. I thought it would be quicker than going back down and joining the path at the bottom, then walking up again.'

'Yeah,' I said. My legs were beginning to scream. The recent storms had made the ground soft and unreliable. What looked like crooks or shelves of hardened soil, protruding out from the mountain, caved beneath our feet the moment we stepped on them. The hill was almost vertical now. The only way to continue was to use the trees as anchors to pull ourselves up, but in places where the trunks were a few feet apart, the scramble became a leap of faith. Yet the only way to get off the mountain was to keep climbing upwards, until we reached a ridge at the top. The ground was less steep up there. If we made it that far, we could walk to the path that connected to the mountain's peak.

I tried to push myself up with my foot, but the ground kept giving way. Beneath me was a twelve-foot drop. The slope's slanted angle meant if I slipped, I would just slide, but if I fell backward, I might just hurtle straight down to the next clearing below. At the very least, I'd have a broken collarbone. I tried to push myself up again. The muck caved underneath, sending me forward into the side of the mountain. I screamed.

'It's okay,' Stu said. He sounded like he was trying to coax an anxious four-year-old. To him, a man of the mountains, this was nothing, but I was spent. Flat ground was somewhere 350 feet below. Exhaustion had crept in around 250 feet above that. Without the ground to propel me forward, I was struggling. My twenties had added a layer of fat round my stomach, and my arms had remained the thin, weak reeds they always were, even with weekly workouts at the local MMA gym.

'Let me grab you.' He reached down, looped an arm through my legs and pulled me up. 'Climb up over me.'

'Will you be okay?'

'Yes, don't worry about me.' A hand pushed me from behind, sending me up further. I clambered up, gloved fingers sinking into the muck.

The lad was going to be impossible to find in this terrain. Stu was right. If you wanted to spare your family or some innocent hiker out for a walk in the woods the trauma of finding a dead body, you'd head up this route. The foliage was so dense that, coupled with the thick grey sky above, winter wardrobe colours like greys and greens and blacks – what he'd been wearing when he went missing – wouldn't stand out. And the climb was challenging enough to distract from the task at hand, especially for volunteers with little mountain experience. If he was here, someone would stumble on him accidentally, if at all, and it probably wouldn't be until the summer. By then, the body wouldn't even be recognisable.

Along with tiredness, shame was starting to settle. I'd become a hindrance rather than a help. This was not a big mountain. Another path up it was somewhat technically challenging even for amateur climbers like Stu, but K2 it was not. Some locals would argue it wasn't even a mountain, just a hill. The idea of having to call for help to get down off it was preposterous. The conditions, though, had made a mildly challenging climb for the fit almost dangerous for the incompetent. And mountains were never to be underestimated, no matter how small they were. The year before, a tourist had gone missing and been found beneath the summit; a gust of wind, she'd said, had toppled her over the nose, sending her hurtling sixty feet down. Somehow, she'd survived the fall. A local high-school teacher had not been so lucky: he'd fallen to his death. Both had gotten into trouble through no fault of their own.

Above me, a rock jutted out from the slope. If I leaped on to it, it might give way, the ground being as soft as it was. In my hand was a thick, broken branch Stu had found and fashioned into a makeshift crutch for me earlier. To get to the rock, I needed to step across a groove of mud that didn't look like it could guarantee secure passage. I went to toss the branch across, over to the next mini-ridge in the mud above, where the rock was. Instead of landing upwards, it fell to the ground below.

Stu snorted.

'Well, that was stupid,' he said, laughing. The ability to see the funny in our current predicament had left me somewhere around the two-hundred-foot mark.

'Yeah, I didn't mean to do that,' I said. 'I was trying to get it over to the other side; I couldn't get across with it.' Hunkered down, I edged across, ready to grab grass, muck, anything, if the ground collapsed.

I threw myself on the rock. The ground started crumbling beneath me again, but somehow I managed to pull myself up.

The ridge at the top of the mountain suddenly became visible. The trees gave way to an open field of overgrown grass.

'C'mon,' Stuart said. 'We're nearly there.'

Every few feet, my legs would give out from underneath me and I'd collapse into the grass in a heap, but unlike the slopes below it was soft, welcoming. If I zipped my coat up, I could curl up for the night or even just a few hours and sleep but the grass was so thick, I feared I could be sleeping on bodies. I could picture them – lying down, tucking themselves underneath the grass and slipping off into the ether. So I got up and kept walking upwards, until we met the path.

'Do you wanna ride on my back?' Stuart asked. 'It'll be like Frodo and Samwise Gamgee on Mount Doom, in *Lord of the Rings*.'

'I'm okay, thanks.'

Mist was beginning to roll in over the summit, along with a promise of rain. We needed to get down quickly. As we descended, the data connection on my phone returned. I checked the Facebook group the volunteers were using to share leads and tips.

'They're saying now he was spotted somewhere else,' I said. 'Over the other side of town, later the day he went missing. After he was seen up here.'

The path down was as slippery as the slope coming up. The mud was as thick as tar, trapping our feet as we walked. My phone buzzed again.

'They're now saying he might have taken his passport.'

'I bet that fucker is in Malaga having a pint, while we've been struggling up here,' Stuart laughed.

I hope he is, I thought.

*

Three weeks later, they found the young lad's body on the mountain. Where they found him, they didn't say. Had we just missed him? Had we walked right past the corpse?

It would have been easy to do, yet the thought was guilt-inducing; him, dead but alone, just a mile or two from home but lying closer to the sky than to the ground. Maybe it was the last vestiges of an Irish Catholic upbringing stirring guilt inside me. Even as the world had changed and technology advanced and my generation began to leave the Church and God behind, every death in the family was met with the same rituals, and one of them was never leaving the body alone. It would be stationed in the coffin, usually in the living room, and family and friends would take turns to stay, snoozing on the sofa or in the chair, making sure the person lying there wasn't on their own for this part of their journey.

Why had I told Stu I'd join him that day? I thought about it in the shower afterwards, as I washed the muck and dirt off. Black and purple bruises had spread across my knees and shins, but otherwise they were intact. Why had I agreed to help Stu when I was so unfit? How could I have helped?

The answers were multiple and conflicting. I knew he was dead but I wanted to find him alive; I wanted to help rule out which part of the mountain the body wasn't on; maybe not finding a body was better than finding one, but what if not knowing was worse for one family than knowing was for another?

Then there were the selfish reasons for doing the search. Searching for the boy had provided an idea of what to expect, of how the hours and days and weeks after someone went missing unfolded.

FOUND

Constitutional Question Is Holding Us Back

Growing up on an interface during a conflict – even one that's fading – means your childhood was not normal. North Belfast was a difficult place to be during the nineties. Knowing where to go and where not to go was a matter of life and death. At eight years old, I knew that venturing too far down Manor Street was a risk; one of the surviving Shankill Butchers was rumoured to live there. Three streets up was Rosapenna Street, where Loyalists would drive down from a nearby road that connected the Oldpark to the Shankill. I was banned from going there after my mum saw a young father murdered.

I lived with the same fears as the other kids. We knew there were certain adults in the street we were to never talk back to. If our football landed in their garden, we ran.

I remember one individual, in particular, who frightened children and adults alike. We were warned to not upset him because 'people who argue with him go missing.'

As I'm typing this, I wonder if my mind has invented it all. I know it hasn't. I'm twenty-four next month. In sixteen years, Northern Ireland has come so far. The contrast between 2014 and 1998 is so stark that the old days don't feel real.

Yet not everyone has moved on. There was uproar this week over an Australian SDLP candidate, Justin Cartwright, who described himself as an 'economic Unionist' in an interview. The *Irish News* was the first to swoop in for the kill, followed by he of Land Rover surfing fame, Gerry Kelly, whose only comment was that Justin was clearly not an Irish Nationalist.

The argument, as it went on Twitter, was that the SDLP is a party whose main goal is a United Ireland. Sadly, Kelly and the SDLP – who made it clear to the *Irish News* that Cartwright had been reprimanded – didn't seem to realise that they were the ones missing the point.

As I said, I'm nearly twenty-four. I'm from a mixed-religion family but was baptised Catholic and grew up in a Republican area. I'm the kind of voter Sinn Fein might target. Yet I won't vote for them or for the SDLP. While they bicker with Unionists and worry about a United Ireland, I'm worried about paying this month's bills. Work is hard to come by. The cost of education – at undergrad and Masters level – is so high that the door has practically been closed on working-class young people. If it wasn't for one regular part-time gig, I wouldn't be able to put myself through university. I've had to adjust to a world in which there is no job security. Meanwhile, the politicians who supposedly represent me are arguing about a constitutional issue I have absolutely no interest in.

The Good Friday Agreement has created a new generation of young people, freed from the cultural constraints and prejudices of the one before. It used to be that being a Unionist or Nationalist was an accident of birth. You didn't decide whether you were for the Union or not; the decision was made for you. Your friends were drawn from your own kind.

Looking at my own social circle, it's clear how times have changed. One of my oldest friends is a DUP-voting Orangeman who marches every Twelfth of July. Another friend is a former Loyalist paramilitary who has tried to make a new life for himself. Another is a former Provisional IRA member who has done the same. Rounding this motley group off is my friend Declan (not his real name), a policeman from a staunchly Republican family.

Just fifteen years ago, it would have been unthinkable for someone like me to have such an eclectic friendship group. It would have been unthinkable for someone like Declan to join the police. Whilst our politicians debate issues connected to the past, we have moved on.

So I welcomed Justin Cartwright's comments. For me, that he considered himself an 'economic Unionist' wasn't significant. What was significant was his willingness to campaign on issues that are actually affecting our society. It was an acknowledgement of what most voters are thinking: the constitutional debate is irrelevant. It doesn't pay the bills. It doesn't get new laws passed. It doesn't improve life in Northern Ireland in any tangible way.

Whilst I saw the tail end of the conflict, I didn't see enough to make me bitter towards 'the other side'. I saw enough that peace and moving forward seemed like the only options. Most children of the GFA generation – those born after 1998 or who were relatively young when the Agreement was signed – saw no conflict at all. Slowly, a common consensus is emerging, the belief that the Union vs a United Ireland argument should be left to die. It's holding us back. It reminds us of days past.

I don't want a United Ireland or a stronger Union. I just want a better life.

Suicide of the Ceasefire Babies

'He's only seventeen, how can he be dead?'

For once, Big Gay Mick wasn't saying much. 'I don't know. We just seen his stepdad getting out of a taxi at the top of the street and he told us.'

There was no getting any other details out of him; he was in shock. Big Gay Mick was not normally lost for words. Stick-thin, with a baseball cap permanently pulled down over his eyes and a gold chain around his neck, you might have mistaken him for one of the neighbourhood hard men until you heard his voice: shrill, camp and a fair bit higher than what it should have been post-puberty. In our little teenage gang, he was the only one brave enough to be openly gay. It wasn't easy.

We grew up just off Murder Mile, a stretch of the Antrim Road so called because of the number of casualties there during the Troubles (the wider area was known as the Murder Triangle for the same reason). On the street where Big Gay Mick lived, beside a 'peace wall' that separated us from the Protestants, Loyalist paramilitaries would drive down, single out a target and pull the trigger. Even though

Mick lived just two streets away from me, I wasn't allowed to go to his until I was ten years old, two years after the Good Friday Agreement – a key part of the peace process – was signed. In an area where murder and mayhem created hardened men, it was not easy to be as camp as Christmas. He managed, though, all the while smirking at a member of the local paramilitary who would shout homophobic abuse at us as we walked by.

The swagger was gone today. I was grilling him and he didn't have the answers I wanted.

'How can he be dead?'

'He killed himself. Apparently he escaped from the hospital. They found him in the grounds.'

I don't remember much of what happened after that, other than walking upstairs, kicking something in the bathroom, and cursing Jonny for dying.

The Ceasefire Babies was what they called us. Those too young to remember the worst of the terror because we were either in nappies or just out of them when the Provisional IRA ceasefire was called. I was four, Jonny was three. We were the Good Friday Agreement generation, destined to never witness the horrors of war but to reap the spoils of peace. The spoils just never seemed to reach us.

The first time Jonny tried to kill himself, the ambulance was parked just beyond his front door, as if the paramedics were mindful of drawing attention to the house. Despite the fact that the local papers brought news of suicides every week – for some reason the numbers had rocketed – there was still an element of Catholic shame about it all. When they carted him off to hospital to pump the tablets out of his stomach, his mother didn't go with him.

That night, he was released. We'd formed a 'suicide watch' in preparation: 'You go in for your dinner and I'll stay with him, and then I'll go in for my dinner when you come back.' When he joined us, little was said. We didn't ask him why he'd done it. He was only sixteen, the rest of us a year or two older. To our teenage brains, suicide was like cancer, an accident of fate. Sometimes people survived it, and sometimes they didn't. The newspapers, bringing reports of more deaths every week, spoke of it like a disease, using words like 'epidemic'. It never occurred to us, as we took turns to keep an eye on Jonny that night, that it didn't matter what we did. He would just keep trying until he managed it.

Jonny was my best mate. We'd met three years before, when his family had moved into the street. My house was at one end of the road; his, the other. We matched in several ways: dark hair, dark eyes and glasses. People mistook us for siblings. But one thing that didn't match was our ability to sing. While I could be outdone on a harmony by a choir of alley cats, Jonny had a voice like velvet. Every day, he'd rehearse in front of the mirror, singing along to CDs, trying to reach higher and higher notes. With a tough home life, the thought of being on stage was what got him out of bed every day. When his mother left the house, he'd bring us up to his room and practise. Sometimes, you couldn't walk down the street without him bursting into song.

One day we were standing at his end of the street. I had a secret to tell him.

'I'm gay,' I said.

'Guess what? I am too!' he replied.

It was a relief to find someone else 'not normal'. We were the neighbourhood's resident freaks – or so we thought. Walking through the area, day or night, was a bit like running over hot coals, except instead of trying to avoid being burned, you were trying to avoid the local hoods, hoping they wouldn't spot you.

There were five of us: me, Jonny, Jonny's brother Jimmy, Big Gay Mick and Tanya, a sweet-natured English girl with long fair hair and blue eyes. But, as childhood friends do, we grew apart. Maybe we'd have grown together again if another ambulance hadn't come and taken Jonny away. His brother told me about it afterwards. It happened at a house party. With a few drinks in him, he'd got upset, disappeared and taken another lot of tablets. By this time, his mother had been taken ill and was recovering in a home. Jimmy had been sent to live with his dad. The last I'd heard of Jonny, until Big Gay Mick knocked on my door, was that he was in a mental health hospital. Now he was dead.

I lived in the street for three more years. When I left, Jonny's house had been boarded up, the windows barricaded with sheets of rusted metal. The only window left untouched was the one at the top, the one through which the neighbours used to hear him sing.

When someone dies by suicide, they leave behind questions. Attend a wake or a funeral in such circumstances and you'll hear them, posed by family members tortured by the big 'Why?' Why did she do it? Why didn't he talk to me? Why didn't she say goodbye?

Those were not the sort of questions that Mike Tomlinson, a professor of sociology at Queen's University Belfast, could answer. What he could do, though, was talk about the broader picture. 'Essentially, the story since 1998, which just so happens to be the [year of the] peace

69

agreement, is that our suicide rate almost doubles in the space of ten years.' From the beginning of the Troubles in 1969 to the historic peace agreement in 1998, over 3,600 people were killed. In the sixteen years after that, until the end of 2014, 3,709 people died by suicide. Contrast this with the thirty-two-year gap from 1965 to 1997, when 3,983 deaths by suicide were recorded. Over the last few years, Tomlinson's research has mainly focused on one question – why?

'Now, that trend [the almost doubling of the suicide rate since 1998] is wholly out of line with what happens everywhere else,' says Tomlinson. He describes a presentation he gave at Stormont, the parliament buildings of Northern Ireland, that includes graphs of the trends in suicide in England, Wales, Scotland and Northern Ireland. 'Of all the presentations I've done in my career,' he says, 'there's an audible gasp from the audience every time I've done that [one].'

It's not that suicide didn't happen before 1998; it did, although researchers caution that it may not have always been recorded as such due to religious norms and relatives' shame. Yet during his research, Tomlinson discovered that of all suicides registered in Northern Ireland between 1965 and 2012 (7,271 in total), 45 per cent were recorded from

1998 onwards. It's the oddest of anomalies: if the official statistics can be taken at face value, more people are killing themselves in peacetime than in war.

In a paper published in 2013, Tomlinson wrote: 'Since 1998 the suicide rate in Northern Ireland has almost doubled, following a decade during which the rate declined from a low level of 10 per 100,000 of the population to 8.6.' The overall rate is now 16.25 per 100,000: 25.24 per 100,000 men and 7.58 per 100,000 women (2012 figures based on three-year rolling averages). In global terms, this places Northern Ireland in the top quarter of the international league table of suicide rates.

Tomlinson identified adults who as children had lived through the worst period of Troubles-related violence (from 1970 to 1977) as the age group that experienced the most rapid rise in suicides in the decade after 1998. It seems obvious that this group, the middle-aged who'd seen the worst of the Troubles, would be affected. But what about teenagers, people like Jonny? We were the Ceasefire Babies.

No matter whether we were old or young, war added new habits to our lives – everyday rituals that wouldn't be so everyday in most countries without war, like not taking your toy gun outside in case a passing Army patrol or police jeep mistook it for a real one and fired. Or watching your feet as you walked to school because the police were searching the area for a suspect device. Or getting hit by rocks that came flying over the 'peace wall' that separated us from the 'other side'. Yet those things were minor compared to seeing someone shot in front of you, as people older than us had done.

The Troubles' survivors would taunt us: how much had we really seen, compared to them, even if we had grown up near an 'interface' where Catholic and Protestant areas met? Yet of the 3,709 people who lost their lives to suicide between 1999 and 2014, 676 of them – nearly a fifth – were aged under twenty-five.

31 July 1972. The day three bombs went off in Claudy, a small village in the Faughan Valley, six miles south-east of Derry City. That day, Siobhan O'Neill's mother left her shop in the village, turning left to walk down the street. If she'd turned right, O'Neill may never have been born.

O'Neill never witnessed the carnage of the Troubles directly. But she saw its effects on people's everyday lives: in the fear of her parents when she told them, aged eleven, that she wanted to attend secondary school in Derry, not the village. Derry, like Belfast, was a hotspot for murder and bombings.

Today, her job largely involves examining the legacy of that violence. O'Neill is a professor of mental health sciences at the University of Ulster's School of Psychology. Last year, she led a team of researchers who established that there is a direct link between suicidal behaviour and having experienced a traumatic event, including those related to conflict.

It was confirmation of what many had long suspected. Of the sample interviewed for the study, just 3.8 per cent of those who'd never experienced a traumatic event had seriously considered suicide. If they'd experienced a non-conflict-related traumatic event (like a car crash, for example, or a loved one dying from cancer), that number jumped to 10.5 per cent. And for those who'd experienced conflict-related traumatic events? The number increased further still – to 14.2 per cent.

What shocked O'Neill even more was her discovery that, out of the twenty-eight countries that participated in the World Mental Health Survey Initiative – including Israel and Lebanon, places with ongoing, bloody conflicts – Northern Ireland was the one whose population had the highest rates of post-traumatic stress disorder (PTSD).

Some 39 per cent of Northern Ireland's population, she says, have experienced a traumatic event related to

73

the conflict. While suicide rates among the middle-aged could, in part, be explained by the trauma of the Troubles, how could the deaths of young people who'd never seen the war be accounted for?

There is no single common factor in suicides among young people, according to O'Neill. Many things can be involved: educational underachievement, poverty, poor parenting. But the Ceasefire Babies are also dealing with the added stress of the conflict – even though most of them never witnessed it directly. 'When one person sees something awful, when one person is traumatised, it will affect how they relate to everybody else, including how they relate to their children, their grandchildren,' says O'Neill.

'People who've been affected by the Troubles live in areas where there's high rates of crime and poverty. When you're a child growing up in poverty, being parented by people who've been traumatised and everyone around you has been traumatised, you are going to be affected by that, even if you've never seen anything. Even if they never tell you the stories.'

At the University of Haifa in Israel, students can take a course called 'Memory of the Holocaust: Psychological Aspects'. Taught by Professor Hadas Wiseman, it outlines how the traumatic experiences of Holocaust survivors have been passed down to their children and grandchildren, a phenomenon known as 'intergenerational transmission of trauma'.

Much research has been published on the subject. In 1980, a husband-and-wife team, Stuart and Perihan Aral Rosenthal, presented their research in the *American Journal of Psychotherapy*. Titled 'Holocaust Effect in the Third Generation: Child of Another Time', it examined how the trauma of Holocaust survivors had travelled down the generations. It should have been a red flag to governments and policy makers across the globe: the effects of war did not stop with the murdered, the injured and the traumatised.

In 2012, another study that looked at the Holocaust, published by researchers at the University of Haifa, confirmed what many academics had argued for years: that trauma survivors pass their behaviours down to their children. A report in the Israeli newspaper *Haaretz* said: 'Survivor parents were perceived by some second-generation children as being inaccessible, cold and distant. And even though these second-generation participants described their parents' inaccessibility as being problematic, some of them were perceived by their own children as being remote and cold.'

Researchers, including Professor Rachel Yehuda at Mount Sinai Hospital in New York, are exploring how the effects of trauma and stress could be passed down to off-spring biologically. Epigenetic changes – alteration of genes in terms of their activity, rather than their DNA sequence – can be inherited, and it's thought these may explain how intergenerational transmission of trauma occurs. In August 2015, Yehuda and colleagues published a study of Holocaust survivors that showed, for the first time in humans, that parental trauma experienced before conception can cause epigenetic changes in both parent and child.

These findings are among the latest in an increasing body of research showing that intergenerational transmission of trauma is not just a sociological or psychological problem, but also a biological one. Could this heritable aspect of trauma explain why so many young people in Northern Ireland, like Jonny, are taking their lives? As the sociologist Mike Tomlinson pointed out to me during an interview, the problem with answering that question is a lack of data. Who are these young people? What are their backgrounds? Where are they from?

Tomlinson recounted a time he was interviewed on the BBC World Service about his research. At the end of the interview, a fellow interviewee from the USA asked him, 'Where is the evidence from other countries?' The problem is, there's very little. In war, the ruling government usually collapses – and with it any form of meaningful record keeping. Northern Ireland was unique: the Troubles was an internal conflict throughout which the state remained strong, even when the mainland was being bombed. To borrow a scientific term, it's the best dataset we have to prove that the problems faced in a war-torn country do not end with the arrival of peace.

Yet the experiences of Northern Irish families in the post-conflict era are playing out in other countries, even if the patterns aren't being recognised. After one presentation at an international conference where he talked about Northern Ireland's soaring suicide rates, Tomlinson was surrounded by people from different countries affected by conflict. 'This is exactly what we see,' they told him. 'But again,' he says, 'it was anecdotal, it wasn't well documented.'

The Sunflower is a tiny little pub perched on a corner in the alleyways that sit between the edge of North Belfast and the city centre. With bright green paintwork, it's known for attracting a genteel crowd of writers, journalists, poets and musicians, a smattering of post-conflict hipsters who wear tight jeans and tweed jackets and Converse. There are poetry readings and concerts by local indie bands in a smallish room upstairs. A sign outside on the wall says: 'No Topless Sunbathing – Ulster Has Suffered Enough'. For tourists, it's an introduction to the natives' quirky black humour, our way of dealing with all that's happened.

For those of us who grew up in North Belfast and know the area, the sign calls to mind the suffering experienced on those very streets when a Loyalist murder gang, the Shankill Butchers, drove around looking for Catholic victims to torture and kill. Yet one night, I end up there, drinking at a table with my Protestant best friend, at least two Republicans and a group of Corbynite socialists. Times have changed. If I'd been born a decade earlier, I wouldn't have dared to venture down those streets, never mind drink there. Now, it's safe.

It was there that I went, one Thursday afternoon, to meet Jonny.

We never figured out why Jonny's stepdad told Big Gay Mick that Jonny was dead. We found out within a day that he was still alive. Now he was sitting in front of me, toned and muscular, with his dark hair swept over his eyes, the glasses replaced by contact lenses. While I'd never really shaken off the unkempt geeky look, he looked like he could have been an extra in a *Baywatch* beach scene.

We'd all grown up together – me, him, Big Gay Mick, Tanya, Little Jimmy – but there was so much he'd kept hidden from us. While we were hanging out, he told me, he would disappear to his room and take a swig of vodka. Drink was easy to get where we lived, even without ID. Between arguments with his stepfather and mother, things had been getting tougher at home. The first time he'd tried to kill himself, he'd walked down to his mum's, picked up a box of pills, swallowed a load and passed out while vomiting.

He'd had depression for a while. 'All I understand it being was sheer despair. It was a despair that you couldn't lift – it stayed with you all day, when you slept, and you woke up and you felt the same way, and you felt the same way when you went to sleep – if you did sleep,' he says. 'It's just a constant . . . I call it "the black dog". It's a constant sort of feeling hanging over you, of just pure "anti-ness", hopelessness.'

After a second suicide attempt, he was taken to a mental health facility. Several more attempts followed. 'I was always very opportunistic – it was never planned out,' he says. 'If I saw an opportunity I took it, so I was quite impulsive, so it was quite frightening. I think I was under observation for a while.' Since then, though, his life has changed. With the help of medication to keep him stabilised, he has his own flat and is going back to school. He still sings. Next year, he plans to try out for a televised singing competition.

I was grateful to be there, in that weird hipster bar, drinking with Jonny instead of visiting his grave. Then I thought of all those who should have been sat there with us – friends and acquaintances who never made it into adulthood. We could have filled the Sunflower with them and still had people spilling out on to the streets. The problem hasn't gone away. On Christmas night in 2015 in Ardoyne – an area in North Belfast that saw thirteen young people kill themselves over a six-week period in 2004 – a young woman called Colleen Lagan died from suicide. She was the third member of her family to take their own life in the past ten months.

Those who survived the Troubles called us the Ceasefire Babies, as if resentful that we'd grown up unaccustomed to the sound of gunfire, assuming that we didn't have dead to mourn like they did. Yet we did. Sometimes, I count their names on my fingers, quickly running out of digits. Friends, friends of friends, neighbours' relatives, the kids whose faces I knew but whose names I learned only from the obituary column. The tragic irony of life in Northern Ireland today is that peace seems to have claimed more lives than war ever did.

Why I Set Myself on Fire at Belfast City Hall – Man at Centre of Horrific Street Protest Breaks His Silence

Grainy video footage shot on a mobile phone of a man trying to set himself on fire in Belfast was uploaded to YouTube and shocked all those who viewed it.

The person filming appeared to be one of a gaggle of teens congregated at Belfast City Hall on 30 April last year.

In the video, they can be heard jeering at a dark-skinned man with curly hair as he douses a rag in some flammable fluid and sets it alight.

'Is that all you're burnin'?' one of them shouts. Another bursts into song: 'This girl is on fire.'

Within a few minutes, however, one of the crowd realises that something is not right.

As her friends tease the man, she can be heard telling one of them, 'No, I can't, I can't do this, see if he's gonna . . .'

They continue to taunt him. When he shouts, 'Fuck the system,' they shout it back at him.

Then the shouts turn to panic as they realise the man intends to set himself on fire. Soon after, the video went viral.

Belfast Telegraph, *August 2015*

In it, a teenager later identified as Paul Russell can be seen grabbing the man and pulling him away from the flames.

The man who tried to set himself alight never spoke to the media about why he tried to do it – until now.

Thirty-five-year-old Faycal Daoud, from Algeria, is homeless. When we meet, he is carrying all his possessions, including his identification papers, in a rucksack.

Since being evicted from his apartment because he could not afford to pay the rent as a destitute refugee, he is entitled to minimal or no benefits and is not allowed to work. He has been sleeping in a friend's office, waking up around 5 a.m. to leave before an employee or the boss arrives.

The incident at Belfast City Hall was, he says, both a protest and an act of frustration.

He fled Algeria in 2008, driven away by poverty and a government that harassed and jailed journalists and critics.

By his late twenties he had already been imprisoned twice, once on conspiracy charges and the second time for assaulting a policeman, which he vehemently denies doing.

Seeing no future in Algeria, he sought asylum in the UK, with a brief spell living in Dublin before returning to the UK.

Refugees can wait for years before being granted the right to stay, as Daoud did.

His application for asylum and subsequent appeal have both been rejected by the Home Office. While he can appeal the decision again, he is currently surviving on the charity of friends.

His friend Josephine Devlin, a Belfast-based community worker, said: 'Making them [refugees] destitute is basically a way of starving them out before they can make another appeal.'

Retired human rights lawyer Padraigin Drinan has also expressed concern about Daoud's case.

Before the incident at City Hall, Daoud was living in a damp-ridden, third-floor flat – conditions he says his doctors argued were inappropriate given his epilepsy and asthma.

Yet constant complaints to the relevant bodies were ignored.

'I found myself in a circle,' he adds. 'I discovered that nobody cares.'

Suffering from depression and feeling isolated, he turned to a number of organisations for help, but just one of them provided him with assistance.

'If the organisations for refugees and asylum seekers won't look after them, who will look after me?' he asks.

'[Other than the one organisation], the only ones who

cared were my neurologist, my GPs, the epilepsy nurse –
they did their best.'

In April 2014, after what he felt was yet another fruit-
less meeting with a charity, Daoud decided he had had
enough.

He said he walked to City Hall with the intention of
setting himself on fire.

'Around 6.30 p.m., it all came to a head,' he says. 'I wasn't
suicidal, but I was angry and suffering from depression. I
just wanted to object [to what was happening to him]. It
was an act of frustration.

'Between living in the UK and Ireland, I've suffered
too much. I've been beaten, I've been threatened. I'm a
human being.' Asked what was going through his head
at the time, he says: 'This is the right time, this is the
right moment, this is the right place to show that you are
frustrated.'

The media, he claims, did not want to know his side of
the story.

'They didn't make more effort to know the reason,' he
says. 'Before any act, there is a reason, so we should let the
other person give his version and not just take one version
of the story.'

He says refugees are suffering and desperate, and that

no one is listening to them. After an Algerian politician called for his brother, a journalist, to be executed for blasphemy over a book he wrote, Daoud is too terrified to return to his native country.

The Ardoyne Festival Has Been Controversial at Times, But the Organiser Is Keen to Break Sectarian Barriers

At first Paul McCusker thought it was fireworks he'd heard. It wasn't a silly assumption. He was standing on a make-shift stage in Holy Cross Boys School pitch, the venue for the yearly Ardoyne Fleadh in Belfast that he helps organise, surrounded by thousands of revellers. The sound of fireworks would not have been out of place. It had been a long time since he'd heard gunshots, too long to remember exactly what they sounded like.

It wasn't the sound of the fireworks, though. Word soon reached the Fleadh team that a young man in his early twenties had been shot. McCusker and a team of first aid volunteers arrived before the paramedics did. It was the festival's final night.

Afterwards, walking back to the pitch, he looked down at the Fleadh hoodie he was wearing and considered whether to hang it up for good.

'I remember walking after the shooting and walking into the pitch where the concert takes place and saying, you know: "Why am I doing this?" Particularly after

Belfast Telegraph, *August 2015*

what actually happened, he was shot in front of kids,' he said.

'When I witnessed the scene, I was down with paramedics, it wasn't a nice scene. So, when I went back on the pitch, I had a Fleadh hoodie and I wanted to take it off and go home, but I know the work I'm doing is very positive. People love the Fleadh, so I said: "No, I'm going to keep on doing it."'

A day or two later McCusker's phone started ringing constantly. It was the media. He hadn't heard the comments made by the Druids, a band who'd played at the event the same night the shooting happened.

During their set they told British soldiers and their 'Orange comrades' to go back to England.

Too often Ardoyne only makes headlines for the wrong reasons: the Twelfth of July parade, dissident Republican activity, shootings. For anyone familiar with McCusker's work, this additional firestorm was hard to watch.

McCusker is, to use a colloquial term, an Ardoyne legend. Using Facebook, he's been promoting the community to people on both sides of the divide, highlighting the work being done by community workers and volunteers, many of whom are teenagers.

As we walk about the area, he is like a proud father as

he reels off the achievements of the young people, even though he himself is just twenty-nine. Volunteering in the community since he was fourteen, under his watch kids from the Shankill's Hammer Youth Club have been visiting the area, working with a team from Ardoyne Youth Club on the Belfast2Blanco project.

Every year McCusker, along with a team of Shankill and Ardoyne youth workers, takes the group on a trip to Blanco, an impoverished township in South Africa. While there they help the local community, doing everything from cleaning the area to feeding the hungry.

The trip was the brainchild of Shankill youth leader Alan Waite and Ardoyne youth leader Thomas Turley. It has created lasting friendships, with young people now travelling back and forth between the Shankill and Ardoyne to visit each other.

He said: 'Religion never came into it, there was no issue in terms of any arguments or anything like that. Those young people were prepared to work together regardless of whether someone was a Catholic or Protestant. It's been one of the big bonuses.'

With the efforts being made to reach out to young people in the Shankill and invite them into Ardoyne, the Druids debacle, he confesses, was 'a nightmare'.

'The Fleadh is very positive and we wanted to keep that, particularly when we had kids from the Shankill over,' he said.

Since then the Fleadh committee has put in guidelines for performers to ensure there isn't a repeat of the incident this year.

Open-air concerts this weekend will see Irish reggae band Bréag and pop act Fusion play, with the Wolfe Tones headlining on Sunday night.

At the end of its press release it says: 'Ardoyne Fleadh is very much welcomed by the people of Ardoyne and we would like to extend a hand of friendship to our Protestant neighbours.'

McCusker gets too little credit for the community work he does – all unpaid and voluntary – while holding down a full-time job as a health worker. As we stand in the shadow of Holy Cross Church, he points to a nearby construction site.

'See that building up the road? That's the Peace and Reconciliation Centre. Community groups are going to use it. There's going to be two entrances – one at Ardoyne, one in the Woodvale. That's where the riots happened [over the Twelfth]. Behind the cameras, all this is going on.'

Ardoyne still has many issues, something McCusker readily admits, from antisocial behaviour to sectarianism. It's one of the reasons he didn't hang up his Fleadh hoodie.

'Still lots needs done,' he said.

Across the road, in the grounds of the church, a car honks and someone shouts. We look across. Two community leaders, one from the Shankill, the other from Ardoyne, are waving at us.

'They must be about to head into a meeting about the centre,' says Paul. We watch as they leave the car together, one in what looks like a Celtic jacket. It's a sight that would have been hard to imagine just a few weeks ago, never mind ten years ago. Ardoyne hasn't changed completely, but thanks to people like Paul McCusker, it is changing – for the better.

The Fight of Your Life

The footage is nearly forty years old but you can see him clearly: pasty, red-haired, more Irish-looking than Italian.

'Some of you may have observed the knee brace on the left knee of Johnny Lira,' says the announcer, Howard Cosell. 'That is occasioned by the fact that there are pellets in that knee. Remember I told you Lira had a troubled youth? The pellets the result of being a participant in a gang war.' He pauses. 'Just recording the fact.'

Lira, a fierce, determined fighter who has previously served prison time, darts round the ring as he and the Venezuelan Ernesto España exchange blows. España's using dark brown Mexican gloves, with stitches sewn in where the leather connects with the skin. In round nine, they will rip into Lira's cheek and tear a gash above his right eye so bad that his face is doused in blood. But he doesn't know this yet. It's only round six.

An evenly fought match up to this point, things start to change in the seventh round. 'And in a round like this, it seems to me, the more polished style of España becomes more visible,' says Cosell.

'Oh! That counter-right by Lira! Knocked España down!'

Lira's friend Fred jumps on the table, screaming, as Al Capone's ex-driver looks on. Ernesto España, the world lightweight champ, bested in the ring by an Italian-American street punk. The first knock-down of the fight.

España gets back up. 'We will not be going to a station break,' Cosell says.

The seventh round counts down: fifteen, fourteen, thirteen . . .

'Lira's got a lifetime at stake here. You can understand the hunger in this young man. Boxing, as I said, turned his life around: the troubled youth, involved in gang wars, involved in crimes and then here he is, fighting for a championship!'

The bell rings.

'There can be no doubt about the scoring in that round. It was Johnny Lira's round.'

But there are more to go.

In the next round, España fights back. He knocks Lira down towards the end. In round nine, both men continue to battle.

'But right there – España got through with the uppercut and you saw Lira's head snap upward! . . . A lot of blood gushing out now! The blood we had anticipated earlier, over Lira's right eye, and Lira is in trouble!'

Watch the scene frame by frame and there it is: the point at which Lira's brain must be bouncing around inside his skull, like a snapped elastic band. Concussion? Howard Cosell doesn't realise it but he's narrating the beginning of the end of Johnny Lira's life.

The ringside doctor stops the match after the ninth round. España is named the winner by technical knock-out.

But that was decades ago. The crowds are gone now. Cosell is long dead. There is no audience. Johnny's screwed. He knows it. He's forgetting things. He's drinking too much. He's paranoid, can't control himself, to the point where, one day, he loses it with the teller in the bank and threatens to blow the place up. His speech is slurred. He's increasingly reliant on the sign-language skills he picked up while training a young deaf boxer he'd spotted in a boxing club one day, David Davis, the Silent Bomber – whose career ended when he was injured in a car crash.

Jerry Lucieno has been Johnny's best friend since childhood. They've worked together, boxed together – when Johnny needed bail money at 3 a.m., it was Jerry he called.

Now they're sitting in Jerry's car, outside Johnny's apartment, sorting out Johnny's affairs.

'What's going to happen to these guys that are pasta brains from taking hits?' Johnny asks Jerry. 'You know, these boxers,' he continues, 'everybody wants to make money on 'em and nobody puts anything into 'em. They just leave 'em at the roadside. And that's not right!'

He's talking as much about his own life as he is anyone else's. His liver is failing. He's sixty-one and running out of time. The boxing community in Chicago rallies round, holds a fundraiser for his medical bills, but when he dies, a few months later, he dies penniless.

When the dangers of boxing are discussed, it's often about what can go wrong during a fight, incidents like the one during Barry McGuigan's 1982 fight with Young Ali that left Ali in a coma from which he never recovered. These risks are still present. In late 2015, Hamzah Aljahmi died in Ohio following his debut professional bout. In 2016, Scottish boxer Mike Towell died after a match in Glasgow, and English boxer Nick Blackwell was forced to retire after sustaining a head injury during a fight.

But the boxers that this story is about haven't died in the ring, but because of it – years later – when the bloodied noses and split lips had long since healed. At the time

Johnny was fighting, it was called 'Punch Drunk' syndrome. Now, it's called chronic traumatic encephalopathy (CTE). And while boxers and their brains were instrumental in the research to define the disease and establish it within medicine, their contribution has, say their families, largely been forgotten.

*

It happens in a small town in western Canada.

It starts years before it ends. Paranoia. Mood swings. Violence.

One night, he forgets where he left a piece of machinery. She talks him through it. They figure out that it must be in the next town, at the site of a construction job. He drives there. He calls on the way: 'I know I'm here for a reason. I have my trailer hooked up to my truck, but I don't know why I'm here,' he says.

Another night. They're having dinner at a friend's house when they receive a phone call. Dayer, their youngest son, has pulled a knife on Caiden, their eldest son, during an argument.*

* Some names have been changed.

They go home.

She, Maryse, asks Dayer what happened. The boy is under extreme stress. A few days earlier, her husband, Curtis Hatch, waited for him behind a corner near their garage, jumped out and tried to smother him. Her nephew saw and came running in: 'Auntie, Uncle Curtis just grabbed Dayer and he's hurting him.' Curtis was an ex-boxer, a three-time national champ; if she hadn't got there, he might have killed him.

Curt walks over and interrupts. He tells Dayer, 'When Social Services get here, I'm going to request that you be removed from our home.'

Dayer runs into his room and begins, literally, to climb the walls. Their nine-year-old daughter wraps her arms and legs around her father and pleads, 'Daddy, please don't do this.'

Maryse snaps.

She grabs Curt's arm and leads him across the kitchen into their bedroom.

'You're going to pack a bag,' she tells him.

'You're kidding me, right?' he says. After the incident with Dayer, he offered to leave. She said no. Dayer told her that he couldn't be in the same house as his dad. She told him it would be okay. He was soon going to go to winter camp for a few days. 'I'll make sure Dad stays away from you and by the time you get back, we'll have some help. We'll have some answers and it will be better.'

Three days later and it wasn't better. She hadn't been able to get help.

'Pack a bag and leave,' she tells him.

He walks over to the walk-in closet in their bedroom. That's weird, she thinks. Does he have a bag in there?

She only realises what he's doing as the gun comes into view. Too late to stop him shooting himself in the chest.

She lifts the phone. She forgets the numbers she's supposed to dial. 911? 411? After what feels like forever, she remembers. The dispatch operator tells her to stay where she is, that help is on the way. Flash the lights on and off, they say. She does. Then a police officer's voice breaks in on the line: 'Get out of the house now!'

The house is a building site: they're still finishing it. There's no porch, so she picks up her daughter and leaves through the garage door. Later, a police officer – their friend, the same person who arrested her husband just weeks before over another incident – confirms that he's dead. She was too shocked to realise she'd heard two gunshots. He'd aimed the second at his head.

The death is declared a suicide, the final act of a man with a history of paranoid violent behaviour. It's a textbook case: a man abuses and terrorises his family, then harms himself or them. Some men are just evil. But Maryse knows different. She knows something was wrong with his brain. She just needs to find out what.

*

Looking at mainstream press coverage of chronic traumatic encephalopathy (CTE), you'd be forgiven for thinking it wasn't a big problem in boxing – searches reveal the names of countless players from the US National Football League (NFL) with the disease, yet far fewer boxers.

The science is in its relatively early stages: we know that CTE affects people with a history of concussion and repeated blows to the head, a group that includes everyone from domestic violence survivors to NFL players. It affects the brain, causing problems as diverse as memory loss, slowness of movement and extreme rage, in ordinary, loving people.

If you follow the logic that CTE is caused by repeated blows to the head, you might expect legions of boxers queuing up to say they have it. They don't seem to be coming forward. Either they've never heard of CTE or they don't want to talk. For the boxers I approached, it seemed to be the latter: 'I don't want to talk about anything that's going to damage boxing,' they'd say. Most others in the field I contacted, including gym trainers and officials, didn't respond to requests for comment at all.

Over time, I began to understand why this might be. Football players have teams of people to look after them, from physicians to nutritionists to agents, as do professional boxers. Most boxers, though, are amateurs. While NFL players have managers taking care of the business side, amateur boxers – at least, those trying to turn pro – have to write to sponsors and other funders themselves. They are salespeople and boxing is a business. Brain diseases aren't good for business and neither is talking about them.

But there's one friend I know I can count on to talk.

'I'm tellin' you, you won't find many victims,' he says, sweeping his hand across thin air, as if to emphasise the nothingness. Marty is nearly six foot tall, with cropped curling black hair, thickening stubble and broad shoulders. Sitting in a cafe in Belfast, he looks as if he is permanently on the verge of grabbing the next passing male and pulling him into a good-natured headlock.

Marty practically grew up ringside: sparring, training, fighting and, now, promoting fights. The sport was good to him: a working-class fella with no qualifications, he left school at sixteen and learned how to do business by watching promoters broker deals and oil the PR machine that amped bouts. It was war turned into theatre. Now, he's an entrepreneur himself, with fingers in multiple pies across the events business. One of his more recent ideas was providing bands to weddings. You can't go wrong with weddings, he tells me: 'Everyone has one and they happen all year round.'

Boxing made him and, as far as he's concerned, the benefits hugely outweigh the risks. He tells me a story: 'I was running a white-collar boxing event and one woman came to me and begged me to let her son in. He'd tried to kill himself multiple times and she had done everything she could . . . I let him in. And you know what? It saved his life.' The training kept him focused, he says, gave him purpose. 'I still see him training in the gym sometimes.'

*

'I'm just shocked that no one wants to talk to us and then suddenly, someone comes from five thousand miles away,' Nina Lira-Santiago says to me. There isn't any great story to tell. An email to Lisa McHale, Director of Family Relations at the Concussion Legacy Foundation – an institute in New England dedicated to advancing research and knowledge of brain trauma in athletes and other at-risk groups – led me to the names of two boxers who'd suffered from CTE.

One of them was Johnny 'World-Class Pug' Lira. In and out of jail in his youth, he'd turned his life around when a judge, Marvin Aspen, gave him a light punishment in return for a promise that he'd focus on his boxing. It had paid off. Now his daughter, Nina Lira-Santiago, is sitting in front of me.

I didn't realise before I arrived, but where we meet, a gym in the basement of a children's home in Chicago, is where greats like Floyd Patterson and Muhammad Ali trained. Pictures of Ali line the walls. Outside, the gym's owner, Glenn Leonard, a six-foot-tall Rocky Balboa look-alike with heavy shoulders, meets me and leads me in. He gave up his boxing career after four or five years of proper competing to work as a trainer. The only time he gets in the ring now is to spar.

'Can I ask why you couldn't fight any more?'

'Aw, well, you know, I was having headaches and, you know, it's a warning signal.'

I turn up expecting just to meet Nina and a couple of other family members but there are already six people inside. By the time I leave, I've interviewed at least ten, including Johnny's sister, who flew in from Salt Lake City for the occasion.

When it comes to Nina's turn, she tells stories about her father as if the memories are like scenes from a disjointed cinema reel. Conversations with him that didn't make sense, that just went round in circles.

She tells a story her younger sister Gina told her: Johnny, a few years before he died, manic, as if he was back in the ring facing an opponent, kicking Gina as she tried to push him out of her apartment door.

It wasn't until Nina rang with a similar story – their father, defiant, in her house, refusing to leave when she'd told him to because he smelt like liquor, offering her a fight – that it came out. 'Dad was not even Dad,' Gina said. 'He looked at me like I was some kind of stray animal on the street, like he was about to beat my ass. I've seen my dad in rumbles. Dad looked at me like I was a dude.'

And then the same thing happened at Johnny's sister Joanne's house, where he had gone to pick up some of his belongings. 'Out of nowhere, he got really violent with her,' Nina says.

Joanne's son came out: 'Uncle Johnny, step back,' he said. 'You need to relax and calm down for a second.'

Days later, Nina spoke to her aunt about what had happened. 'I've never ever been afraid of your father,' Joanne said. 'Until that time.'

And then there was the bank. Thinking that his sister and his bank were trying to take his money, Johnny asked to withdraw it all, threatening to blow the building up in the process. 'We know what his temper's like,' Nina told a relative at the time, 'but this is something different. He's a ticking timebomb.'

The 2015 film *Concussion*, starring Will Smith, is loosely based on a series of true events. It tells the story of the study of CTE in NFL players by a Nigerian-born forensic pathologist called Bennet Omalu, and the League's refusal to accept his findings.

In 2002, the body of an ex-NFL player, Mike Webster, arrived in Omalu's office in Pittsburgh. An examination of Webster's brain revealed something unusual. 'I had to make sure the slides were Mike Webster's slides,' Omalu told PBS *Frontline* in a 2013 interview. 'I looked again. I saw changes that shouldn't be in a fifty-year-old man's brain, and also changes that shouldn't be in a brain that looked normal.'

Viewers of the movie would be forgiven for thinking that CTE is an NFL problem and an NFL problem alone.

Indeed, modern interest in the disease has tended to veer towards the NFL and the relationship between CTE and American football. But the first known description of the disease was in boxers. It came from a New Jersey physician, Harrison Martland, who described the condition in a 1928 journal article called 'Punch Drunk'. In 1937, another doctor, J. A. Millspaugh, named the condition dementia pugilistica. It's now accepted that this is a type of CTE.

It's not clear how many boxers the disease affects. But the accumulation of brain-related trauma from each fight leads over time to the release of a protein called tau, a common denominator in brain-related diseases, including Alzheimer's. It spreads through the brain, eroding the functions associated with affected parts.

NFL players get concussion because of the blows to the head they sustain when charging at each other on the field. A study from the Cleveland Clinic in Ohio showed that even sub-concussive hits – blows to the head that don't cause concussion – can lead to significant brain damage for an athlete in the long term. Yet, in boxing, the very aim of the game is to land a blow to the head of your opponent. If anyone is at risk of the disease, it's boxers – so why haven't we heard more about them?

'The bottom line is most of these boxers are poor,' says Nina. 'They have a lack of education, their families have a lack of education, so they can't advocate for themselves.

'I've had so many arguments with certain research groups, telling them that in terms of spreading awareness about CTE among boxers, they need to be going into deprived communities because that's where they are. We've talked to the boxing authorities too but . . . I don't know,' she says. 'I worked in public health; I know that the funding is there to make this happen. But there seems to be a lack of will.'

*

I think I'll be fine until I walk in and see the sign on the metal doors that reads, 'Feet first, head by door.' I can feel the blood drain from my face. Then one of the student interns lifts a brain out of its container and I have to choke down the vomit that has started to rise to the back of my throat.

'I don't mind brains,' says Don, the cheerful PR guy overseeing my visit. We're standing in a morgue at a VA hospital (for veterans) on the outskirts of Boston, a picturesque estate of rolling green fields and trees with buildings plopped in the middle. It belies the state of the mostly male population of residents inside, who've been injured by wars from Vietnam to Afghanistan. 'I saw one when it was still in somebody's skull, in Iraq; he'd just had his head blown off.' He says it so casually, I suspect he saw a lot on his tours of duty.

Ann McKee arrives, glasses perched on the end of her nose, pulling on her white lab coat as she walks. Several critics have expressed dismay that McKee wasn't featured in the movie *Concussion*. An article in *Wired* said, 'It's a bit strange that the story centers on Omalu when Ann McKee at Boston University has been doing this research for just as long . . .'

But it's McKee's name the families remember. When their loved ones' brains are collected from the local morgue and sent to Boston's CTE Center, it is her lab they end up in. It is she who dissects the tissue and, along with a colleague, rings each family to confirm that the reason the person they knew and loved had changed to, in some cases, a violent abuser was CTE.

When brain sections are stained for the protein tau in the laboratory, it shows up as dark brown patches. McKee keeps boxes in front of her desk, with labels like 'NFL players, aged 51–100'. In small glass cases, she has samples of their brains which she shows to visitors, documenting the erosion of their life: brown, discoloured stains on the tissue which manifested themselves in the form of rage, fear, paranoia, memory loss and confusion.

McKee takes me back to 2003, when her story started with a boxer called Paul Pender. A Marine veteran, he was a two-time world champion who'd fought Sugar Ray Robinson. Twenty years after his boxing career ended, when he was in his fifties, his personality had started to change. He'd become depressed and irritable, eventually unable to hold down his job. 'That was when he first came here, to the VA, to be evaluated and even though it didn't seem typical, the diagnosis was Alzheimer's disease.' He subsequently developed memory problems and confusion.

'When he died, I was doing the autopsies and I fully expected to see Alzheimer's,' she says. 'But he had anything but.' For one thing, his brain lacked beta amyloid plaques – another kind of protein that has to be present for a diagnosis of Alzheimer's. And while tangles of tau protein are seen in both Alzheimer's and CTE, in CTE the tau tangles are always around blood vessels.

'He had a brain that . . . for a person who studies brains and makes that their life mission, I'd never seen anything like it. The tau pattern in this particular brain was extraordinary.'

McKee tried, fruitlessly, to find the brains of other boxers. Then, one day, a brain turned up from someone who had also been diagnosed with Alzheimer's. 'I said, "Wow, this looks like Paul Pender's brain."' She couldn't see any history of boxing in the records, but called the family herself. 'Did he ever do anything unusual or were there any sports he played?' she asked. Yes, they said, back in his twenties he was a professional boxer.

'The symptoms of the disease don't often begin until many years after the person stops having exposure to repetitive head impacts,' says McKee's colleague Robert Stern, from his office in Boston University's main campus. 'It's something about that repetitive exposure to head impacts – whether they're symptomatic, like concussions, or non-symptomatic – that turns on the disease.'

The symptoms are insidious, creeping. As the disease progresses, Stern says, it affects a person in a number of ways. Their cognitive capacities, like memory, judgement, and planning and organisation skills, can falter. Their mood and behaviour can change, with a risk of apathy, depression, mood swings, rage, aggression and loss of self-control. And they can also develop problems with motor functioning: stiffness or slowness of movement, tremors and limited facial expressions. 'What's interesting,' he says, 'is that [limited facial expressions] have always been a common part of what's seen in boxers but we very rarely see it in American football players. We're trying to figure that out.'

From research based on interviews with families and friends, and by looking at medical records, Stern and McKee know that there are two types of patients with CTE: those who initially present with behavioural issues, usually in their thirties, and those who initially have cognitive problems, typically beginning in their fifties, sixties and seventies. But it's not clear why some boxers develop the disease and others don't.

'I don't think many people will argue that smoking [doesn't] cause lung cancer,' says Stern. 'But does that mean everyone who smokes will get lung cancer? Obviously not … [It's the] same thing with repetitive head impacts. Some people with that history seem to get CTE. Not everyone.'

But everyone who has ever had the disease has one thing in common, he says: a history of repetitive impacts to the brain.

'I used to say we're in the infancy of our scientific knowledge of CTE,' says Stern. 'Now I think we're in the toddlerhood . . . we still don't know a lot.' The biggest problem facing researchers is that the disease can only be diagnosed post-mortem. Until they figure out how to diagnose CTE during life, he says, they can't do the kind of studies that will give them these answers. It's the current focus of his research.

*

'I can tell it's taken its toll on me,' he said to Jerry. 'I can still feel the punches sometimes.' A few months after their conversation in Jerry's car, Johnny Lira was dead. The obituaries talked about the 'World-Class Pug' and the almost world champ. None mentioned the reality of the later parts of his life, such as the slurred speech or the inability to control himself or his drinking.

While some members of Johnny's circle – and even Johnny himself at times – had begun to suspect that something was wrong with his brain, it was only after his death that his daughter, Nina, could fully connect the dots. An examination of his brain by McKee confirmed he'd been suffering from CTE.

A few months after Curtis's death, Maryse Hatch was in Salt Lake City when she came across an interview with the widow of an NFL player, Shane Dronett, who'd been diagnosed with CTE after his death at age thirty-eight. Like Curtis, in the years leading up to his death he'd become unusually paranoid, thinking that people were driving around the house and following him. Again, like Curtis, he'd died of a self-inflicted gunshot wound.

'She said, "He had gone into the kitchen and as soon as I put my hand on the front door I heard it," Maryse remembers. 'And when I read that the first time I was like . . . I could physically see her husband, I could see the look in his eyes. Everything. I just read that and I knew. Whatever he had, that was the same thing [that Curt had].'

She emailed Boston University. Luckily, the coroner in Canada had saved three pieces of Curtis's brain, which they sent to Boston at her request. 'I was so sure there's something wrong with Curt even though we knew it was a suicide,' she says. A full autopsy at her request hadn't found anything. Then, in November, the phone call came from Boston.

'It was literally a gift,' Maryse says. 'To be told. To understand . . . I'd been so angry at him and I can let some of that go.'

Knowing the truth about why a man changed so terrifyingly can help a family to mourn, to remember him the way they loved him. And the fans remember too. In a museum, thirteen miles east of the town where Maryse and Curtis lived, there's a small Sports Hall of Fame. In the section for 1993, there are nine photographs in brown frames. In the middle of the bottom row is a black-and-white shot of a young man in a white vest who's looking straight down the lens, his fists raised in a fighting stance. Below it says: 'Curtis Hatch. Born February 1, 1970. Athlete – Boxing.'

Bigger Issues than Tribalism Being Ignored and No One Seems to Care

The latest statistics from the Electoral Reform Society showing that just 4 per cent of Catholics would give their first preference vote to a Unionist party and 2 per cent of Protestants to a Nationalist candidate could be interpreted as depressing.

They suggest that voters haven't moved away from tribal notions of identity. Birthright, not belief, it seems decides what way voters swing. Yet, is it a bad thing if Catholics and Protestants stick with their traditional constitutional positions?

The default position among those in the 'middle ground' is yes, and until two or three years ago I would have agreed with them.

A childhood spent growing up near an interface had taught me to loathe any form of tribal allegiance. Republicanism and Unionism/Loyalism were, for me, inevitably intertwined with conflict, hatred and an aversion to progress.

Yet, the reality is that neither Unionism/Loyalism nor Republicanism is inherently bad.

Belfast Telegraph, *February 2017*

The problem is how they're interpreted or applied.

The old line about a Bible in one man's hand being as bad as a whiskey bottle in another's springs to mind.

To say that Catholics and Protestants sticking with their traditional constitutional positions indicates a lack of civic progress is to ignore how their political beliefs are rooted in culture and community.

Being a Republican/Nationalist is about more than wanting a United Ireland, as is being a Unionist or Loyalist.

Each comes with its own set of traditions, culture, ties, even language and dialect – and to expect people to abandon that in the name of 'progress' is both short-sighted and an impossible bar by which to measure progress against.

Worse, it plays into a broader, unhelpful narrative that pits Unionists and Nationalists against each other. It suggests that, as long as people subscribe to either, the peace process is a failure, because the two cannot peacefully co-exist.

It's this assumption that our politicians – and our country – seems to operate on: that the conflict hasn't ended and there's still an enemy that needs to be defeated, and they're living on the other side of the peace wall.

Yet, that's not true. And as long as we believe it is, we're setting the bar pretty low for how we expect our public representatives to behave.

The peace process will not be a failure because we did not abandon our political beliefs or cultures. It will be a failure because we did not learn that each other's existence is not something to be objected to. The reaction to Mike Nesbitt's vote transfer proposal – which has, frankly, been sickening – shows that this belief is alive and well.

A United Ireland will not happen without a sizeable chunk of the Unionist population consenting. Nor will the sky fall in because Mike Nesbitt gives a second preference to the party he wants to govern alongside.

My fears for Northern Ireland don't lie in tribal differences, but in bigger problems that get lost in the never-ending debate about identity: our spiralling suicide rate, young people who think dying is an option, but a life lived in Northern Ireland isn't, our abysmal lack of mental health facilities, a job-creation strategy that focuses on creating minimum-wage call centre roles that crush the souls of our youth and sends them scurrying for other shores. The peace process delivered peace and nothing else for my generation. We're still dying, even though the conflict is over. And no one seems to care.

Want a Career in Investigative Journalism? Become an Entrepreneur

Recently, a young journalist asked me how he could become an investigative reporter.

The news industry has changed so much in the last ten years that there is no longer a single answer to that question. If you asked me, 'How do I become a lawyer?' I'd tell you to go to law school. With muckraking, it's not as simple as that. To answer that question, we need to consider the industry and what it looks like right now.

The Background: The Media Industry Has a Meltdown

When I left school in 2006, there was a standard career path into journalism: get work experience, pass your degree, sit your NCTJ exams and get on a training scheme. By the time I got to university in 2008, that was no longer an option.

If the digital disruption of news showed us one thing, it was that investigative journalism never had a business model (exceptions such as *Private Eye* and *I. F. Stone's Weekly* aside). It always came as part of a package, bundled with other news. Its survival was dependent on the prosperity of traditional media. In many ways, 2007–8 was our dotcom crash.

Five years on, nothing's changed. We've just shifted the dependency from corporate owners to philanthropic funders. I've said this before but for me, that's dangerous.

Last October, I had the pleasure of sitting in on a meeting between US investigative non-profits and a funder. The funder said something both interesting and scary (I'm paraphrasing from memory but this is the gist of it):

'When are these non-profits going to be sustainable? Cos my guys are looking to pull out of funding them within the next five years.'

The Journalist as Entrepreneur

Opportunities within traditional media to do investigative reporting have also shrunk.

So when young people ask me, 'How do I become an investigative journalist?' my reply is: 'Become an entrepreneur.'

Let me clarify what I mean by that. The stereotypical image of entrepreneurship – ruthlessly capitalist, for want of better words – is completely incompatible with the spirit of public service that embodies investigative journalism. Yet that's not what being an entrepreneur is about.

Being an entrepreneur is about creating value and getting someone to pay for it. So, combining investigative journalism and entrepreneurship simply means producing investigative journalism and getting a customer to pay you for it. Publishing startup Matter is a great example of this.

With most investigative sites choosing to chase philanthropic funding over finding a business model, it feels like we haven't had a proper discussion about investigative journalism's future and entrepreneurship's role in it.

'Going it alone' is now a necessity for making a living – not just in journalism.

It's the same across the creative industries. Musician Jerry Klickstein wrote a brilliant post on the need for music schools to teach entrepreneurship:

The music education community is swirling with talk about how best to prepare university-level students for modern-day careers. And for good reasons. The music business is undergoing economic and technological upheaval, and many musicians and colleges are struggling to adapt. Actually, some musicians appear to be thriving – those with entrepreneurial mindsets . . .

Entrepreneurial musicians find multiple outlets for their talents. For them, loving music and making a living from music are one thing. Like Isaac Stern, they adopt ways of life that bring both fulfillment and income. For example, a professional saxophonist I know combines teaching, performing, and recording with a penchant for technology; among other things, he's developing music education apps for the iPhone. Similarly, a Juilliard-trained violinist felt the tug of rock music and then built a career as a rock violinist while also presenting hundreds of school workshops and launching a successful line of electric violins.

In sum, entrepreneurial musicians don't wait for job openings to appear. They make opportunities by forming broad artistic visions, expanding their skills, and generating demand for their work.

Size and Scale: Launching a Micro-Enterprise

I tried the entrepreneurial route once before. Some readers may remember that I was the co-founder of a company called NewsRupt. We built an app called Qluso, an online marketplace where investigative journalists could sell their work to editors.

It ended disastrously.

The problem wasn't the product. Eventually, we could have made it work. The problem was that my heart wasn't in my work.

My idea had started off as a radio production company. I wanted to be an investigative reporter who made radio documentaries. That was it.

But I was broke and needed some money to get things started. So I talked to some investors who told me my idea was all wrong. It would never 'scale'. If I wanted to be in business, I needed to build a product, a web service perhaps.

They were partly right. If you want to build a huge business, build a product, not a service.

But if you want to make a nice living doing something you love, you don't need to think about building something millions of people will use. If a few hundred people like what you do, that's enough to make money from it (the hard bit is working out *how*).

People in startup circles tend to forget that. Startup blogs worship companies that make lots of money or sell to bigger companies. They confuse success with making lots of money. Having bought into the whole 'Let's build something and sell it for millions of dollars!' bull, I can say that success is doing something you love and getting paid for it. If more journalists could figure out how to make £20–40K a year just off their reporting, the industry would be in better shape than it is now.

You don't need to start something huge. You just need to start something you love.

Who Is Going to Pay for the Future of News?

I've been asking myself this question a lot lately. *The Muckraker* costs money to run and those costs are going up. Right now, it's funded out of my pay check but sooner or later, I'll need to pay volunteers and stop dipping into my own funds. I don't mind covering the costs but I can see the day coming where server costs will conflict with my ability to eat.

The truth is, the scoops we publish are worthless. A day after publishing a huge story, every paper in Northern Ireland (or the UK if it's big) will have copied it. You won't need to visit *The Muckraker* to read it; Google News will give you a selection of free versions to pick from. That's how the web works. It gives us choices. Paywalls seem silly to me.

Still, I think people will back *The Muckraker* in whatever way they can.

What newspaper publishers don't understand is that paying for news is no longer an economic transaction. It's an act of love.

When people backed Andrew Sullivan, they weren't doing it because the *Dish* provides them with news they can't get elsewhere. They were doing it because they love him and his perspective on the news.

I backed *Homicide Watch* on Kickstarter even though they don't cover Northern Ireland. Why? Chris and Laura's story touched me. I'd never met them, yet, through Twitter, I could see them sitting at their kitchen table every night, typing furiously, helping grieving families by reporting on the death of their loved ones. How could I not back them?

Amanda Palmer summed it up best in her recent TED talk, 'The Art of Asking', when she stressed the importance of connections. Sometimes, all you need to do is ask people for help.

Contrast this with the attitude of newspaper publishers as they erect paywalls. They're like bailiffs, threatening to cut readers off from the flow of information if they don't pay up. Yet that information can be found in a thousand different places across the web. Those who do pay up are doing so out of love.

Northern Ireland's Leaders Still Can't Agree on One Big Issue: How to Deal with the Past

Northern Ireland's two biggest parties, the Democratic Unionists (DUP) and Sinn Fein, announced on Tuesday that they had come to a new agreement to save the power-sharing assembly at Stormont from collapse.

In an agreement titled 'A Fresh Start', the two parties laid out how they would deal with issues such as welfare reform, which has yet to be implemented in Northern Ireland, and contentious parades – a huge issue as the Orange Order stages countrywide marches every year on 12 July.

Yet there remains one huge issue they are unable to agree on, and which has consistently destabilised all Northern Ireland's previous fresh starts since the Good Friday Agreement: how to deal with the past.

More than three thousand people were killed during Northern Ireland's thirty-year war, known as the Troubles. The relatives of the dead have continued to demand justice, never giving up hope that there will be prosecutions for the murders of their loved ones. It's a partisan issue in NI that frequently divides the parties.

Buzzfeed, *November 2015*

For example, the DUP's members would be against prosecuting the Bloody Sunday soldiers, while Sinn Fein's would be for it. Equally, Sinn Fein does not want the former IRA volunteers within its own party to be prosecuted.

Complicating all this is the lack of a clear definition of who qualifies as a 'victim'. Does an IRA or UVF volunteer who died on 'active service' – i.e. while planting a bomb or en route to shooting someone – meet the criteria? Their families say yes; their victims say no.

And then there's the residual bitterness left by the conflict. Across the divide, many voters view the lives lost in their community as tragedies but the lives lost in the other community as collateral damage. It's a classic case of 'one man's terrorist is another man's freedom fighter'.

It makes consensus on how to deal with the past a political landmine for politicians. The victims themselves are divided on how best to approach the issue: some are in favour of an amnesty, others want to see their loved ones' killers do jail time. The biggest issue stalling movement, however, is that the NI secretary of state, Theresa Villiers, will be able to veto the contents of any report by the new Historical Investigations Unit (HIU) on grounds of national security.

The HIU is the new unit being set up to investigate Troubles-related murders. Families engaging with the body will receive a report summarising what's known about their loved one's murder, similar to how the HIU's predecessor, the Historical Enquiries Team, worked. Villiers' veto power is troubling for a number of reasons – mainly for families whose loved ones were killed by British state agents or where collusion is suspected.

Many murders during the Troubles were carried out by double agents, members of paramilitary groups who were secretly working for British intelligence as informers. Director of Public Prosecutions Barra McGrory recently announced he'd instructed the chief constable of the Police Service of Northern Ireland to launch an investigation into British agent and IRA member Freddie Scappaticci, reviewing up to twenty murders.

With regards to collusion, David Cameron admitted in 2012 that British security services and police had colluded with Loyalist paramilitaries in the 1989 murder of Belfast lawyer Pat Finucane. However, Finucane is believed to have been just one of many such victims.

And this is what makes Villiers' veto a difficult pill to swallow for NI's political parties. If an investigation were to be launched into Pat Finucane's murder or a murder carried out by Scappaticci, for example, there's a good chance the families of the victims would never see the HIU's findings.

It's hard to see how this impasse is going to be resolved. Sinn Fein especially cannot be seen to give in to the British government on the issue, as most victims of collusion came from the Republican/Nationalist community they represent. Unionist victims are also unhappy with the veto, meaning there's a cross-community lobby of dissent.

And no party wants to be the one seen as 'selling out' victims, especially with assembly elections approaching next year; the tales of horror from the Troubles are so heart-rending that any move against victims' interests results in extremely bad PR. Shelving the issue of the past while ushering ministers back to their seats in the executive could sow the seeds for yet another stalemate.

Requiem for a Journalist

Yesterday, I received an email from Lise Olsen, an investigative reporter at the *Houston Chronicle* (via the Global Investigative Journalism Network's listserv). In it, she implored the global community of investigative reporters to take action following news that one of our own was murdered in Mexico.

An excerpt:

So it is really important for us AS A COMMUNITY OF INVESTIGATIVE REPORTERS to react strongly to the news this week of an assassination of a young online editor in Mexico [Jaime Guadalupe González Domínguez] – who lived minutes from America – and of yet another armed attack on *El Siglo de Torreon*, one of the most important and few remaining strong voices for press freedom in Northeast Mexico, which has been devasted by violence.

Every time I tweet news like this, I say, 'It could happen to any of us.' Really, what I'm thinking is it could happen to me. And I know others are thinking the same thing.

I'm working on a story that requires me to ask questions about dangerous people. Every day, I wonder if they're going to find out and do something about it.

When I walk to the shop at night, I keep one eye on the road in case a car slows down. Parked cars make me nervous, as do men in hoodies. I rehearse the moment in my head – escaping as bullets whizz past, hiding behind a hedge and firing back with an imaginary gun that I don't own. I know that if it happens, it won't go down like that. It'll happen quickly and I will either live or die.

In reality, my fears are probably groundless. So I tell myself. I know these people have killed before. I pray that they won't kill a journalist, that doing so would raise too many questions – that they're smarter than that.

Yet if they did, how would my 'community' react? What would they do about it? Would they tweet, 'So sad, could happen to any of us'? Or would they actually do something?

Where Is the 'Community' of Investigative Reporters?

Even with organisations like IRE and GIJN (who both do awesome things), I'm not sure we have a 'community' of investigative reporters – not in the true sense of the word.

We don't regularly interact with each other as much as we should.

Let me give an example: NICAR. NICAR stands for the National Institute of Computer-Assisted Reporting. It's a training institute run by Investigative Reporters and Editors (IRE) and the Missouri School of Journalism. A community of news technologists has sprouted up around it. As well as holding a yearly conference, its members are constantly chatting to each other – exchanging tips, asking for advice – via the NICAR listserv. Every day, I get at least five emails. If you asked me to ID its members by Twitter handle, I could probably give you twenty to thirty names.

Could I do that with my own community? No. Beyond a few 'big names', I couldn't give you a list of names the way I could with NICAR. I could name a few but not enough.

That needs to change. With networks like Twitter, there is no reason for us not to be actively collaborating and helping each other.

Requiem

I didn't know who Jaime Guadalupe González Domínguez was until yesterday. I wish I had. We lived thousands of miles apart and spoke different languages. Yet we had so much in common. We both run small, independent news sites. We were both trying to make a difference by exposing the truth.

The last line of Lise's email struck me:

'And do not hesitate to reach out to Javier and others who are subject to these attacks via e-mail, twitter or facebook and tell them personally that – WE as investigative reporters stand together.'

With her permission, I'm publishing her email.

Dear IRE Friends –

I recently wrote for an upcoming book a summary of many recent attacks on journalists in Mexico – and how these attacks have specifically and repeatedly have [*sic*] targeted newspapers and media companies that have most supported investigative reporting and investigative reporting teams particularly in northern Mexico. With a new President taking over in Mexico, I and others were hoping the bombings of newspaper offices, and assassinations of journalists might stop. So it is really important for us AS A COMMUNITY OF INVESTIGATIVE REPORTERS to react strongly to the news this week of an assassination of a young online editor in Mexico – who lived minutes from

America – and of yet another armed attack on *El Siglo de Torreon*, one of the most important and few remaining strong voices for press freedom in Northeast Mexico, which has been devasted by violence.

Here's what you can do and why you should act.

What has happened:

Siglo de Torreon, one of the most important voices in Northeast Mexico, has continued to be the subject of armed attacks DESPITE police 'protection.' *Siglo* requested assistance AFTER its offices were twice attacked by gunmen and after a group of its journalists were kidnapped. This week, Javier Garza, a respected editor, active member of the Interamerican Press Association, a voice for press freedom and one of the prominent speakers at IRE's border workshop in Laredo, said that police made things WORSE [because the officers became additional targets]. (read more here: https://knightcenter.utexas.edu/blog/00-13140-police-protection-attracted-more-aggressions-said-editor-mexican-daily-el-siglo-de-tor)

Meanwhile, the editor of a much smaller online only publication was shot dead in Ojinaga, which is only minutes from the Texas Big Bend border town of Presidio. The attack killed 38-year-old Jaime Guadalupe

González Domínguez. Our friends – including IRE members and former conference speakers at *El Diario de Juarez* – are reporting about how the gunmen used special bullets in the attack to ensure this editor's death. Hours later, the website went dark . . . It has become common for idealistic journalists in Mexico who believe in freedom of the press to fight violence and censorship via their own websites – and they are isolated indeed.

What you can do is SHARE this information with the writers and editors on your editorial page. And if you or your editor or publisher is active in CPJ [Committee to Protect Journalists] or IAPA [Inter American Press Association] or RSF [Reporters Without Borders], urge him or her to take action and write letters. Or, if you are able, write letters or cover this yourself.

And do not hesitate to reach out to Javier and others who are subject to these attacks via e-mail, twitter or facebook and tell them personally that – WE as investigative reporters stand together.

Lise M. Olsen
Investigative Reporter
Acting Deputy Projects Editor *Houston Chronicle*

Decades After Northern Ireland's 'Troubles', Families of the Dead Are Still Seeking Answers – and Taking the Investigations into Their Own Hands

The first bullet pierced Joseph Murphy's leg and exited the other side as he was running across the grass, away from the gunfire. On the aerial map of a field in Belfast, Northern Ireland, which hangs in her office, Janet Donnelly, Murphy's daughter, can pinpoint the exact location where it happened in August 1971: a red pin, marking the spot where he was shot, then cried out to his friend, 'Dessie, I'm hit!' and fell. Dessie's location is marked nearby, a green pin. Green is for survivors.

The second bullet entered Murphy's open wound as he was lying in the army barracks, where the British soldiers brought him, along with the rest of the injured. One soldier stood over him and cocked a gun at his bleeding leg. He fired. This time, the bullet lodged.

Donnelly can point to the barracks, or any other place on the map, and recount what happened there as if she was an eyewitness.

The death of Murphy and ten other civilians during 9–11

From the website Narratively, *published 30 May 2017*

August 1971 would become known as the Ballymurphy Massacre. It was one atrocity of many that would take place during Northern Ireland's conflict, the Troubles, a war fuelled by hostility between the country's Protestant and Catholic factions. By '71, it had only been raging for over two years, with another twenty-eight to go – and thousands of lives to be lost along the way.

This is the British Army's version of what happened that August: members of the Parachute Regiment moved into Ballymurphy, a small area of West Belfast, to round up suspected members of the Irish Republican Army (IRA) and intern them. Rioting broke out, and the troops were fired on. They fired back. Those killed were IRA gunmen, including Father Hugh Mullan, a Catholic priest, and Joan Connolly, a mother of eight.

But while lying in the hospital, Murphy told his wife a different story: rioting had indeed broken out in the area, and he'd gone out looking for their teenage sons. The Army had suddenly begun firing at civilians, all of them unarmed. He was hit in the leg. The soldiers brought him back to the barracks where they beat him and the rest of the injured. One fired a fresh round into his open leg wound.

He died nearly two weeks later from a burst artery.

'One news report said, "The hardcore of the IRA has been wiped out tonight,"' remembers Donnelly.

'It was a bigger injustice than being shot – to have their names ruined,' she explains, her voice rising to a cry. 'Them people were called IRA gunmen when they weren't. I know the truth but when I'm dead and gone, my grandchildren are going to read the stories and think their great-grandfather was a gunman, and he wasn't.'

For nearly twenty years, Donnelly has been trying to prove her father's account. She started, along with family members of the other dead, by tracking down witnesses and taking statements.

In the years that followed the end of the Troubles, many people like Donnelly became amateur cold-case sleuths, trying to get the truth about their loved ones' deaths. Many felt let down by the professional detectives tasked with doing so, like the Historical Enquiries Team (HET). Set up in 2005, the HET's job is to investigate the more than three thousand unsolved murders linked to the Troubles. As always, the catch was in the small print: when a family receives the HET's report on their loved one's murder, the opening lines state that they have 'reviewed' the original police investigation to see if there were any opportunities for follow-up. Almost always, there were not.

Nearly twenty years since the signing of the Good Friday Agreement, a key milestone in Northern Ireland's peace process, many of those left behind by the dead feel largely forgotten.

*

One Wednesday morning in February 2017, some of these family members gathered in a building situated opposite a graveyard near Belfast city centre. Seated alongside ex-prisoners curious about the conflict they'd been caught up in as younger men, they were there to try to find answers, with the help of the clean-shaven, bald-headed man sitting at the head of the table, who had already been through the process himself.

Just over forty-five years before this meeting, Ciarán MacAirt's grandmother had been killed in one of the worst atrocities of the Troubles, the McGurk's Bar Massacre. McGurk's had stood just blocks away from where this meeting was now taking place before it was blown up. Fifteen people were killed in the explosion and seventeen more injured, including MacAirt's grandfather. The bomb had been planted by paramilitaries loyal to the British, but in the days, weeks and years that followed, the British Army would insist it had been an IRA 'own goal'. The IRA, they insisted, had been assembling the bomb on the premises when it went off. The implication was clear: the pub was an IRA haunt, frequented by members or sympathisers. Nobody cared enough about alleged terrorists to demand answers when they were murdered. So when the Army was faced with awkward questions about civilian deaths, they would spin the line that the victims were not so innocent.

MacAirt and Donnelly are a generation apart – he the grandson of a victim, she the daughter of one – yet they were bonded by the same gnawing sense of injustice. They championed each other's work, lending private and public support.

MacAirt's investigation, trawling through ancient public records, unearthed forensic reports that revealed the truth about what happened at McGurk's, leading to an official investigation by the Police Ombudsman. Now, through his charity, Paper Trail, which he founded in 2014, he hopes to impart his research skills and knowledge to others.

'Do you wanna go round the table and introduce yourselves?' he asked.

The five people did so. Today, they would learn about public records laws and archives, and how to mine them for information.

Back on the other side of the city, Donnelly sat in the makeshift investigative unit she'd created specifically for the purpose of investigating her father's murder. Despite recently landing a huge break in the case, she has never been satisfied, and between her duties managing accounts for a community trust, she'd nip back to her office and pore over old files, searching for an angle she may have missed. She's been searching for around twenty years, yet the work is never done and won't be until there is an official independent investigation into her father's murder.

'One witness told us the soldiers had broken into the local butcher's shop and taken knives,' Donnelly says, rifling through a filing cabinet as she talks, looking for a document. Every time she imparts a new piece of information, she reaches for her files – for a soldier's statement, a report – and searches for the exact line that proves she's telling the truth. It's as if she's afraid of not being believed, and so she speaks in a clipped, encyclopaedic tone, only referring to the facts she can prove – like a cop, investigating the murder of someone she's never met.

She'd thought the witness must have imagined the break-in. There'd certainly been rumours about it, but she'd dismissed them after speaking to one of the shop's employees. He hadn't been working there that day, and had assumed that if there'd been a break-in, he'd have heard about it. Then the HET uncovered a statement from a soldier saying they had indeed broken into the shop to take shelter.

'My daddy had sutured wounds – like long, deep cuts – on his body,' she says. 'We don't know where they came from. He was the only victim not to have photographs taken during his post-mortem.' She doesn't say that the soldiers cut him with stolen knives, because she can't prove it happened – but the possibilities of what might have hang in the air.

She managed to track down everything from soldiers' statements to the Army's official investigation into Ballymurphy – 'It's half a page long' – to inquest papers. 'The only thing I couldn't find was my daddy's medical reports [from when he was brought into the hospital],' she says. 'We were told they'd all been destroyed.'

Through paperwork retrieved from the coroner's office, she established that no guns, spent cartridges or bullets had been retrieved from the scene. Gunpowder residue had not been found on any of the victims. She'd discovered one victim was a serving soldier himself, married to a local woman. He'd been visiting the area when he was injured. Another was a British Army veteran.

Joseph Murphy's father, Donnelly's grandfather, had been a British Army veteran himself, having served in the First and Second World Wars. Even after Joseph's murder, Donnelly's mother insisted on helping soldiers wounded in the local area. She'd told her children that as their father and the rest of the injured and dying lay in the barracks, one young soldier had fought with his colleagues, insisting they summon a doctor and a padre (a Catholic chaplain). He was hit with the butt of a rifle. Donnelly searched for him, without luck, wanting to thank him for what he'd done and what he'd tried to do for her father. The HET indicated to her they'd found him; when they'd spoken to him, they said, he'd broken down. For security reasons, they couldn't disclose his identity.

While a lot of survivors didn't find the HET helpful, Donnelly did. They weren't able to provide everything she asked for, but they did give her what they had, including two depositions from her father's doctors. In one, Dr Alan Gurd, who at the time was a consultant surgeon in the Royal Victoria Hospital, detailed his examination of Murphy. Two lines caught her eye: 'On examination, there was an entry wound on the upper aspect of the right thigh and an exit wound on the medial aspect . . . The bullet lying in the symphysis pubis was not removed.'

There it was. The smoking gun, or rather, the smoking bullet.

Inspired by Donnelly and MacAirt, other victims are now using the paper trails of the British government's records to piece together what happened to their loved ones. From intelligence reports by Army officials to correspondence between civil servants, they've found puzzle pieces that had previously been missing.

'The people who attend our workshops are from every walk of life,' said MacAirt. 'They are ordinary families whose loved ones were snatched from them. They are former combatants from paramilitary groups and state forces who are seeking to learn more about the context of the conflict that enveloped their lives. They are academics and researchers with a passion for our shared history. All have a story to tell. We offer them the means to tell their own story in their own words and supported by historical evidence.'

For some, the process didn't just provide justice – but healing.

'The Paper Trail workshop was the first time I opened up about my father's death,' said Stan Carberry. 'We sit round a table [at the workshop] and somebody's father could have been in the UVF [a Loyalist paramilitary group], somebody else's in the IRA, whatever – but we all understand each other's grief.' Carberry's father, Stan Carberry Sr, an IRA volunteer, was shot dead when Stan was eight. He'd been driving a stolen car when the Army fired at the vehicle and missed. According to witnesses, Carberry got out of the car with his hands held out, but was shot and killed anyway. The Army disputed this, claiming he was firing a weapon while he drove the car, although a gun was never recovered from the car, says the younger Carberry. After years of asking questions on his own, Paper Trail helped Carberry discover that the gun used to kill his father was one frequently converted for use by Army snipers. Last week, he attended a court hearing at which the Ministry of Defence revealed what information they held on the murder. 'Every victim is different – some want prosecutions – but I don't,' he says. 'I don't care about the soldier who did it. I just want to know what happened to my father. I've never had a Christmas I enjoyed since my last one with him.'

*

The day they exhume Murphy's body is steel grey. Donnelly is standing in the graveyard, watching from afar: a tent erected around the grave site, to give the body privacy. It's taken two years of legal battles to get to this point; eventually, the coroner granted the family's request to have the body lifted and examined. It was evidence, they'd argued.

Within half an hour, she receives the call. They found it: a military-issue bullet, which, unbeknownst to Donnelly, had been sitting in her father's coffin for forty-five years, embedded in his leg. Joseph Murphy was telling the truth, and his daughter can finally prove it.

The bullet boosts the family's call for an independent investigation into what happened in Ballymurphy in August of 1971. It's a breakthrough, but there is still a long road ahead. And time is running out to hold any of the British soldiers to account; the youngest are now in their sixties at least. Yet there's some hope. Recently, a three-month inquest into the shootings was set for September 2018.

For survivors like MacAirt and Donnelly, the fight for truth and justice is a war in itself. 'Most victims who dared to hope that the likes of the Historical Enquiries Team or Police Service of Northern Ireland would offer fair investigation and truth recovery were gravely disappointed,'

MacAirt says. 'Many have since died. So, it has been up to family members themselves, the great work of NGOs and battling lawyers, to fight for the truth.'

REMEMBERED

A Letter to My Fourteen-Year-Old Self

Kid,

It's going to be okay.

I know you're not feeling that way right now. You're sitting in school. The other kids are making fun of you. You told the wrong person you had a crush and soon, they all knew your secret. It's horrible. They make your life hell. They laugh at you, whisper about you and call you names. It's not nice. And you can't ask an adult for help because if you did that, you'd have to tell them the truth and you can't do that. They can't ever know your secret.

Life is so hard right now. Every day, you wake up wondering who else will find out your secret and hate you.

It won't always be like this. It's going to get better.

In a year's time, you're going to join a scheme that trains people your age to be journalists. I know the careers teacher suggested that as an option and you said no, because it sounded boring and all you wanted to do was write, but go with it. For the first time in your life, you will feel like you're good at something useful. You'll have found your calling. You'll meet amazing people. And when the bad times come again – FYI, your first girlfriend is not 'the one' and you will screw up that history exam – it will be journalism that helps you soldier on.

In two years' time, you will leave school and go to a local technical college. Don't worry – you're going to make friends. These will be your first real friends in semi-adulthood, the people who will answer your calls at four o'clock in the morning. In the years to come, you'll only keep in touch with Gavyn and Jonny but you'll remember the others fondly. When you're seventeen, you'll tell them your secret and they won't mind. It will take courage but you will do it. Gavyn will become Christian and you will fear that he will hate you, but one afternoon, you'll receive a text message saying: 'This changes nothing. You'll always be my friend.' Accept him for what he is as he has accepted you.

You'll go to university, like you always planned to, but you'll drop out because it reminds you of school where people were cold and you had few friends. The campus is just too big and scary. But this experience will be the making of you. You'll be making your way in the world for the first time. Through this, you will meet the people who become your best friends. They'll help you replace all the bad memories with good ones. For the first time in your life, you will like yourself.

Three months before your twenty-first birthday, you will tell Mum the secret. You will be sobbing and shaking and she will be frightened because she doesn't know what's wrong. Christmas will be just a couple of weeks away. You have to tell her because you've met someone you like and you can't live with the guilt any more. You can't get the words out so she says it: 'Are you gay?' And you will say, 'Yes, Mummy, I'm so sorry.' And instead of getting mad, she will reply, 'Thank God you're not pregnant.'

You will crawl into her lap, sobbing, as she holds you and tells you that you are her little girl and how could you ever think that anything would make her love you any less? You will feel like a prisoner who has been given their freedom. You will remember all the times you pleaded with God to help you because you were so afraid, and you will feel so foolish because you had nothing to worry about.

You will tell your siblings. No one will mind. Mary will hug you in the food court in Castlecourt as you eat KFC together and tell you she's so proud of you. The others will joke about how they always knew. They will all say some variation of 'I love you,' 'I'm so proud of you,' 'This doesn't change a thing.'

You will feel so lucky. You watched James get thrown out of his house after coming out to his parents. You were in Michael's house the night his mum said she would 'beat the gay out of him'. You will feel guilty for being the lucky one and getting it easy in the end, even though you went through hell to get there.

You will fall in love for the first time. You will have your heart broken for the first time, and you will feel like you might die of the pain. You won't. You will get over it.

Right now, you're wondering if you'll ever be 'normal'. You are normal. There is nothing wrong with you. You are not going to hell. You did nothing to deserve their hate.

Life will not only get easier, it will get so much better. You will walk down the street without fear. Teenage boys you've never met will not throw things at you and shout names. Your friends will be the best anyone could ask for. You will be invited to parties. You will have a social life. You will be loved. People will use words like 'awesome' and 'cool' and 'witty' to describe you, and you'll forget the times the other kids said you were 'weird' and 'odd' and a 'lesbo'.

You will do 'normal' things. You will spend time with your mum. You will go to work and pay your bills. You will go to the cinema with your best friend every week because that's your ritual – dinner then an action movie where things explode. You will fall in love again. You will smile every day, knowing that someone loves you as much as you love them.

Keep hanging on, kid. It's worth it. I love you.

The Ceasefire Suicides

For me, the year 1998 is bookended by two events. The first one will stand out in the minds only of those who lived through it or were directly impacted. In the twenty years that have passed since, I haven't heard it mentioned again.

Technically, it happened in 1997 – in the last three hours of the year. The local New Year's Eve revellers had gathered in a bar called the Clifton Tavern. It sat on the corner of Clifton Crescent and the lower Cliftonville Road itself. It was a newish addition to the street, sitting beside the local Chinese takeway – which was run by a fierce but pleasant Chinese lady who was more than a match for the mid-night drunks, and her good-natured husband – the local pharmacy and the corner shop.

I can't remember if the Chinese was open that night. I can't remember hearing gunshots either. It must have all been over in a matter of seconds: some time around 9.07 p.m., said a *Belfast Telegraph* report. Loyalist gunmen had stormed the bar and sprayed it with bullets. In hind-sight, it was an ominous scene: a sea of sirens lighting up a dark blue sky, with the light from the street lamps adding an eerie glow to it all. The clock hadn't yet struck 12 a.m. on a new year and here were the police, cordoning off what we would later hear was officially a murder scene after it was confirmed one man had passed away from his injuries. According to Lost Lives, he died minutes before midnight. He was an innocent civilian, caught in the wrong place at the wrong time.

The second event was the Omagh bomb. The collective gasp of revulsion from voters – both Protestant and Catholic – confirmed to those who'd voted 'Yes' in the referendum that they'd done the right thing. Maybe the adults had become desensitised to violence – or maybe they'd been lured into a false sense of security by the peace deal – but there was something about the images from the newspapers' coverage and the UTV bulletins that day that was different.

We'd seen atrocities a thousand times, but the outrage over Omagh was palpable, and it extended from homes in Ardoyne to the Shankill. The majority had voted for the Good Friday Agreement because they wanted the senseless violence to end. Omagh, as I remember it, served only to harden their will.

Because that was why we wanted peace, no? To stop mothers being robbed of sons, daughters, husbands? To stop the violence from visiting our doorsteps, if it hadn't already? Twenty years on, the peace process has succeeded – in some ways.

People are no longer dying at the hands of paramilitaries, but they're still dying, too young and too soon. The culprit now is suicide.

According to a report in the *Guardian* in February, around 4,500 people have died by suicide since the Good Friday Agreement. It's the most tragic of ironies that twenty years of peace could rob us of more lives than thirty years of war did.

Researchers such as Professor Siobhan O'Neill, a world-renowned expert on conflict and suicide who works at Ulster University, have established that there is a link between these deaths and the Troubles. 'We have found that people who witness violence or who have been involved in violence are more likely to act on suicidal thoughts,' she says. 'They are more likely to die on the first suicide attempt because they choose more violent methods.'

Yet the impact of the Troubles in this respect is not limited to first-generation survivors, she cautions.

Trauma can be passed down; the so-called Ceasefire Babies, who did not witness the violence of the 1970s or

'80s and have lived in a time of relative peace, are now suffering from the legacy of a conflict most of them know little to nothing of. Theirs was a generation promised peace, prosperity and a life free from the terrors faced by their parents and grandparents. I can't help but feel that we've failed them.

In the BBC report on the Clifton Tavern shooting, there's an ominous line: 'About a sixth of all the 3,200 victims of the conflict since 1969 have died in north Belfast.' Now, in peacetime, the area is suffering all over again, losing its young people to suicide in droves.

It's horrific enough to lose one child, but some mothers in this corner of the city have lost two or three children. Tragedies of this proportion should have been left behind with the Troubles but, twenty years after the Good Friday Agreement, we're still carrying the coffins of the young to their graves.

Meanwhile, with Stormont not in session, the strategy for preventing these deaths – called Protect Life 2 – is currently languishing in some civil servant's desk drawer. Apparently, it can't be signed off until we have a government.

Yet the evidence, says O'Neill, shows that around 70 per cent of people who die by suicide had not approached any mental health services. What would our suicide figures drop to if we could remove the stigma of saying 'I don't feel okay', so that people can make an appointment with their GP about their mental health as casually as they would if they had the flu?

What if we accepted that as a post-conflict society, we are more vulnerable to mental distress than our peers on the mainland, and treated mental ill health as a normal affliction that comes with having seen and survived conflict or having been born within a generation of it?

News of another death reaches me nearly every week. Again and again, I see the same theatre play out. Statements of condolence from politicians have become as meaningless as the 'thoughts and prayers' offered after every mass shooting in America. Northern Ireland is a country where activity tends to be confused with progress, but make no mistake: until the suicide rate is reduced to as close to zero as we can get it, the peace process has failed the very ceasefire generation it was meant to save from slaughter.

Normally, these – the final paragraphs of any piece I write – are where I deliver some pithy one-liner or (try to) sum up my argument. Yet I didn't write this article to advance an opinion or start a debate. Instead, I want to make an appeal to you, reader. I've talked here about people who are at risk of suicide – who are just not sure if they can go on. Maybe that person is you. If it is, please keep reading – I just want two minutes of your time.

In the last five months, I've lost two good friends to suicide. To protect their families' privacy, I'll call them James and Roisin.

In the months since their deaths, I have felt like grief is eating me from the inside out. I am wracked with guilt. I've spent so much time talking about mental health and encouraging others to talk about theirs, yet I didn't realise just how much my own friends were suffering. Suicide is a thief. It will rob you of the opportunity to see the day when things start to get better, before slowly torturing the loved ones you've left behind. People tell me not to blame myself for my friends' deaths, but I do. Not a week goes by when I don't think of all the missed chances, times when I could have talked them out of it, if only I'd realised what thoughts were in their heads.

If I could turn back time, I would go to the small flat where James lived. I'd beg him not to leave us. I'd tell him how much we love him and that I know he's suffering but we'll fix it and we'll get him help and we'll make things better. Then I'd go to Roisin's house and do the same. I'd beg them both to keep living because I've seen the devastation their deaths have caused.

But I can't turn back time. I can't bring them back. I can only use this opportunity to beg you to reconsider what you're thinking about doing. If you are feeling the same way they did, please, ask for help. Talk to someone. There are amazing volunteers at Samaritans ready to take your call. Talk to your family, friends, neighbours, GP – someone out there will listen. If you feel you have no one, find me on Twitter and ask me to follow you for a private message – I will give you contact details for professionals who can help.

There's a saying within the LGBT community: 'It gets better.' It's what we tell LGBT youths and others who are currently journeying through Hell. Keep going, we say, because one day you'll wake up and be glad that you lived. That piece of advice applies to all of us who are struggling. So please, I beg you – live. It really does get better and you deserve the chance to enjoy it when it does.

Picking the Right Stories to Investigate

I recently came across an old post I wrote about stories I was working on. It was an interesting read because, in the twelve months since, three haven't materialised (the fourth story is being published soon).

Why did they disappear off my radar? I know it wasn't because I followed them up and they all led to dead ends. I plan to return to at least one in the future. Still, I questioned myself about why I didn't put more effort into pursuing them.

Figuring Out What Motivates You to Be Your Best

In the early days of *The Muckraker*, I didn't know what motivated me as a reporter. I just knew that, since the start of my career, certain stories turned me into a workaholic monster. I'd become so obsessed that I'd work all night, eat little and generally never switch off. I'd start working at 10 p.m.; the next time I glanced at the clock, it would be 4 a.m.

These stories had two common themes: 1) Injustice and 2) A need for someone to right the wrong.

The Muckraker, *May 2013*

Why do these stories motivate me? I ended up having this conversation with Farset Labs co-founder (and my friend) Bolster. He summed it up best:

'Growing up, you felt like you got screwed over, that there was a lot of injustice. So now, whenever you see injustice, you try and fix it. You're kinda like Robin Hood without the tights, except you can't fire a bow and arrow for shit.'

He was spookily accurate, right down to the Robin Hood reference. Since the age of three, Robin Hood has been one of my idols (I was devastated when I learned that he wasn't actually a talking fox). He was awesome. He saw the poor suffering at the hands of the rich and *did something about it*. I wanted to be just like him when I grew up.

For me, reporting for the sake of reporting is not enough. It must lead to a greater outcome than publication of the story.

Figuring out what motivates you is key to becoming a good investigative reporter. Ninety per cent of investigative reporting is staying up late to make that extra phone call. You'll only work that hard for a story if it matters to you.

Belfast Telegraph, *October 2016. This was written when Daniel and Amy McArthur of Ashers bakery in Belfast refused to make a cake with a slogan supporting same-sex marriage.*

Fight for Equality Is as Much a Battle for Hearts and Minds as It Is for Legislation

The last time I remember being this confused by an issue was when I realised I had a crush on women and wondered why that was. Eleven-year-old minds aren't very good at comprehending these things.

Undoubtedly, my life from the age of eleven to twenty – when, three months short of my twenty-first birthday, I came out to my mother – has been made more difficult because of religion.

Specifically, Christianity.

My memories of the ages of thirteen and fourteen are of sitting in my bedroom, praying to God that He wouldn't send me to Hell for something I couldn't help and believing it was better to be dead than to be openly gay.

This was the message I took from the Scripture drilled into me via the education system – not that Jesus loved me, but that I was some form of mutated humanity.

I didn't know that my mother couldn't care less about

which gender I dated because, to me, there would only be one reaction – disgust.

I'm no longer afraid of Hell because even if it exists, I've already walked through it.

So, confronted with the McArthurs, my initial reaction was one of rage.

They represent the culture and ideology that I blame for what I and countless other LGBT people have been through, from psychological torture to physical abuse – and I know LGBT people from good 'Christian' homes where their 'Christian' parents believed the only way to deal with a gay child was to beat the gay out of them.

But then, the other part of my conscience speaks up – the journalist who believes in freedom of speech and conscience and asks, 'What about those principles? What about defending the rights of your enemies to speak?'

And so, I yo-yo between the two angels on either shoulder.

In the past I've let my inner demagogue speak because it's easier to feel righteous than to sit down and listen to someone whose views I don't like.

There is a part of me that wants Christians to pay for what happened to me and my people.

Then I look at the history of Northern Ireland and how far that mentality has gotten us, and satisfying that desire doesn't seem like such a great option.

I don't really know what the answer is. Recently, I read a story about an American white nationalist, Derek Black, who renounced his views after building up a friendship with a Jewish student who invited him to a weekly Shabbat dinner, despite knowing who he was, in order to get to know him.

I thought of my friend William, a sweet, rural Christian who is against equal marriage. 'You know,' he said to me, as we sat in a cafe one day, 'I wasn't too sure about you when we first met. I was like, you know, she's gay. But now I think you're a decent wee spud.'

The fight for equality is as much a fight for hearts and minds as it is a courtroom battle.

This case has been exploited by extremist Christians for propaganda purposes, to frighten congregations across the country, creating ill feeling between them and the LGBT community.

If there is one thing I'm certain of, it's that this helps no one.

It doesn't help the man who just wants to worship in his pew, the gay teenager living in fear of Sunday sermons and the might of God, or the bisexual woman with Christian parents.

LGBT people are your brothers, sisters, uncles, nieces, cousins.

Christians are that also.

Then there are LGBT and equal marriage-supporting Christians who have found themselves caught in the crossfire.

Maybe it's time to take the fight to dinner tables, places of worship – anywhere conversations can be had and new friendships formed.

If I could sit down with the McArthurs tomorrow, I wouldn't tell them I hate them, because I don't.

I'd just want them to know that I'm just like them and that, if God exists, I'm fairly certain He loves me, too.

Tweet Suggests that LGBT People May Finally Have a Friend within the DUP

Over the years I've had plenty of rows on Twitter with evangelical Christians and the DUP members, mostly about marriage equality. I've written heated words in this very newspaper. The one thing I've learned is that you can't shift people from their positions by shouting at them. I've tried. Does. Not. Work.

I've yet to hear someone say: 'Wow, that guy on the internet called me an asshole and now I accept he was totally right, and I was wrong!' If anything, the rhetoric of the internet – divisive, bitter, nasty – hardens people and make them stick to their position even more firmly.

Equally, I've seen how conversations can force people to go on journeys. Maybe someone in their family comes out as gay; maybe they meet a gay person and become friends with them. Somewhere along the way empathy makes it impossible to hold on to the beliefs they previously held about LGBTQ people. These journeys always start with a baby step. So, I welcomed the tweet from the DUP's MP for South Belfast, Emma Little-Pengelly, wishing the LGBT community a happy Pride on Saturday.

Belfast Telegraph, *August 2017*

Some said it was a cynical move. Others said it wasn't enough, given the DUP's record of LGBTQ rights. I saw something different. I saw someone who has probably been quietly having conversations with LGBT people and their allies and is starting to change their mind – or perhaps has changed it already. To me, Emma's tweet was brave. She is in a party ruled by the evangelical right: they will be sharpening their knives for her as I write. Yet she hit the send button anyways, when it would have been safer for her to say nothing.

Many equal marriage supporters think that if we can simply drive away the DUP, the equal marriage vote will pass. It probably will – for the moment. The problem with progress, though, is it can be undone in an instant. Look at what is currently happening to trans people in Trump's America.

The rights that LGBTQ Americans believed had been fought for and won under the Democrats are now being rolled back by Republicans. To make progress permanent we need to win the hearts and minds of those who oppose us, otherwise our rights will depend on the electoral fortunes of the politicians that support us. The minute they lose, we lose – and what we lose will be much bigger than an election.

Winning the hearts and minds of our enemies means allowing them to come down from the positions they previously held. Trevor Lunn of the Alliance Party did not support equal marriage. Yet, as he wrote in this newspaper, he reached a point where he could no longer reconcile that position with evidence. We shouldn't berate him for not joining us quickly enough; we should be grateful that he was brave enough to change his mind.

Arlene Foster does not give a damn what lefty liberals on the internet think. She does, however, care what her party members and voters think. We need allies within the DUP – people who will pressure the party to change and advocate on our behalf.

We need people like Stuart Hughes, a young, heterosexual UUP activist who has fought with his party colleagues and tried to persuade them to back equal marriage.

The only people who can change the DUP's stance are its members and voters. I believe people can change. I don't know for certain that Emma is going on the journey that Trevor did, but I hope she is and that, one day, she'll publicly declare that she's had the same change of heart.

How Uncomfortable Conversations
Can Save Lives

There are people in the world who if they're telling you a story need to tell you nineteen other stories first before they can get to the point. I'm one of those people. I want to tell you a story about a conversation I witnessed in a mosque which changed my life. But to tell you that story, I have to tell you another story first. And that story starts in late night, early June, this year. I got the opportunity to go on a trip to the United States with a delegation from around the UK – I was the only one from Northern Ireland – and we were going there to learn about 'American values'. We were going to be travelling across Washington, Florida and Texas, meeting with everyone from guns rights lobbyists to religious leaders and LGBT groups, people who spanned the spectrum of American values. So the thing about these trips is they offer you a number of perks. They offer you carrots they can dangle in front of you whenever the going gets tough, when you are in the hundredth meeting of the day with someone whose views you find absolutely reprehensible and you're really struggling to stay the course. In our case, they took us to Disneyland, which I can confirm

This talk was presented at TEDxStormontWomen

is definitely one of the happiest places on earth. I was in my element. Then they took us to NASA, which, as a Star Wars nerd, I have to say, competed in my heart for the title of Happiest Place on Earth. Someone very helpful pointed out to me – because I was posting selfies of myself at that time, running around Florida in vest tops – that I seemed to have more vests than Rab C. Nesbitt. [*Laughter*] I know the theme of the conference is 'bridges': I felt like burning that one, to be quite frank.

We got to go to this beautiful beachside resort called Cocoa Beach and sip cocktails on the beach; it was absolutely wonderful. You're probably thinking, 'Where do I sign up for this trip?' 'This sounds amazing, it's a free jolly!' That's what I thought it was when I looked at the itinerary. But I had to go through hell to get these perks. I realise that Disneyland and NASA, that these were all carrots they were dangling in front of us whenever I found myself less than ten feet away from the chief orang-utan in the White House. [*Laughter*] *El* Trump. People ask me, 'What's the hardest thing about standing ten feet away from Donald Trump?' I think it was seeing how badly his fake tan was applied. [*Laughter*] I did redeem my conscience when I got to Florida, I should say, and we met these lovely protesters, who, in case you can't see, are holding a 'Stop

Trump' sign. They were right up my alley; I thought they were fantastic.

Our next visit was to a place called the National Rifle Association. It is all the guns rights lobbyists who come out in the wake of every mass shooting and defend the right of Americans to bear arms. For a number of people in the group this was the most difficult part of the trip. They found it very difficult to sit there and listen and exchange views, which was what the whole trip was about.

For me, though, the hardest part of the trip was when we got to Orlando and they told us we were going to be visiting a mosque. Now you ask yourself, why would I find it hard to visit a mosque? Well, for those of you who don't have Gaydar, I'm gay – don't worry, you can laugh, it's okay. [*Laughter*] I hated myself for much of my life because of what religion taught me about people like me. And when I stopped hating myself, I started hating religion. But I was intrigued by this mosque because it was in Orlando, and a year to the week that we were in Orlando forty-nine people were slaughtered in a gay nightclub called Pulse. This mosque had led the response to that tragedy and had condemned it. I was intrigued by that. This was at a time when Christian churches in Orlando were refusing to bury some of the dead because they were gay. To have a mosque come out and condemn this was a big deal. One of the victims of Pulse that always stuck with me was Brenda Marquez McCool. She was a woman who was out with her gay son that night in Pulse, supporting him. When the gunman unleashed his bullets, she threw herself in front of her son. He survived but she didn't. So I decided that I would go into this mosque with an open mind.

I did, and we met with this lovely man called Bassem, who was one of the leaders in the mosque. We talked about everything, and eventually Bassem and I had a conversation about LGBT rights and what Muslims think of gay people. A difficult, thorny subject, we had a really pleasant conversation, but neither of us knew what was about to happen next. There was a young man on our trip who I'll call Mahmud, a young Muslim man. He was listening to the exchange between Bassem and I, and when we were finished talking, he spoke up and addressed Bassem. And he said, 'My best friend was gay, he was Muslim, and he committed suicide.' And at this point, Mahmud burst into tears. He said, 'I did everything I could to save him, but I couldn't.' And he told us this story of how this young Muslim man couldn't live with being Muslim and being gay; he felt that the only option he had was to die by suicide. We were all crying in the mosque, I think, by that point. We were all mourning for this young Muslim man that we had never met and now that we would never get the chance to meet.

You know, when I left religious education at sixteen, I swore that I was done with religion and I was never going back to it. I was never going to have another conversation that I could not help with another person of faith again. When I was in that mosque that day, and I was there to learn about American values, I ended up getting schooled on my own culture by a Muslim. Because I realised that I couldn't run away from religion any more. Within the LGBT community, we have a saying that we tell people. We tell them that 'It Gets Better'. What I realised that day was that it gets better for some of us; it gets better for those of us who live long enough to see it get better. I realised that I couldn't run away from religion any more, because religion shapes how LGBT people are treated in the world. It shapes the laws and how they treat LGBT people, which we can see from the lack of equal marriage in this country. And it shapes how we, LGBT people, feel about ourselves.

The first lesson I learned about being gay was that it was evil and that I was going to Hell for it. I learned that from the Bible. There were times I would cry in my bedroom as a teenager, bargaining with God, asking him not to send me to Hell, because I was so convinced that I was going there. This text, this Bible, I know for so many people it offers them hope, it offers them salvation, but for me it offered a prison sentence. I think it's the same for a lot of other LGBT young people. LGBT suicide rates are through the roof. This [48 per cent] is the percentage of trans youth alone in the UK who have attempted suicide over the course of the last year and before. We see these numbers play out in Northern Ireland locally, and we know this from trans youth services, who say they see it play out among their young people. What do we do about this? I feel the only answer is to change religious teaching of homosexuality and LGBT issues. I don't mean we berate Christians and shout at them or berate Muslims and shout at them.

We need to do the one thing that I didn't want to do when I left school at sixteen: we need to have conversations, difficult conversations, and fight for the hearts and minds of those who oppose us. I've studied this, and when you ask people like Megan Phelps-Roper, who was a member of the Westboro Baptist Church, a hate group in America, when you ask people like this, when you ask former neo-Nazis, the most extreme people, when you ask, 'What changed your mind? What made you abandon your views?' they'll tell you the same thing: it was a conversation. Someone who they were opposed to struck up a conversation, and they learned that that person was not who they thought they were, and they got to a point where they could no longer hold those views. People tell me this isn't going to happen; there's no way the churches will change their teachings or the mosques will change their teachings. 'You're mad.' And I would have agreed with them.

But six weeks ago, I was out in a gay bar – not this one – with my friend Jordan. He's from a Free Presbyterian, DUP-voting family from 'County LegenDerry'. I avoid that Londonderry–Derry thing, I hate that. We were out there with his mum, who is a Scottish Free-P who goes to church every Sunday, and she was out in this bar, supporting her gay son, just like Brenda Marquez McCool was out in Pulse that night supporting her gay son. Don't tell me there's no hope because for too many LGBT young people, that is the only thing they have that keeps them living. And by the way, that Free Presbyterian mother went into work the next day and told everyone about this amazing thing she'd been to called a 'drag show'. [*Laughter*] Now if you had told me that I'd be sitting in a gay bar with one of Ian Paisley's disciples drinking cocktails, watching a drag show, I'd have told you you were mad. [*Laughter*]

What can you do? If you thought you were here to listen passively to me rant on, no, I've got a job for you all. If any of you are uncomfortable with the thought of someone like me, please come up to me after this event and talk to me. I won't bite your head off, I won't call you a homophobe. We'll just have a conversation, and I'll show you that I'm human just like you. If you are comfortable with the thought of someone like me, have a conversation with someone who isn't and try to change their mind. Because you could be saving a life. Finally, I'd like to send a message to all LGBT young people that are currently struggling, especially those from faith backgrounds. "'For I know the plans I have for you,' declares the Lord, "plans to prosper you and not to harm you, plans to give you hope and a future." Jeremiah 29:11. This talk is in memory of the Pulse forty-nine and all LGBT people who died by suicide. Thank you very much, folks. [*Applause*] [*Cheers*]

Notes

SUICIDE OF THE CEASEFIRE BABIES

'3,709 people died by suicide': Northern Ireland Statistics and
    Research Agency: suicide statistics for Northern Ireland:
    http://www.nisra.gov.uk/demography/default.asp31.htm
'Since 1998 the suicide rate in Northern Ireland has almost
    doubled': M. Tomlinson, 'Dealing with Suicide: How Does
    Research Help?' Northern Irish Assembly Knowledge
    Exchange Seminar Series 2013, http://www.niassembly.gov.uk/
    globalassets/Documents/RaISe/knowledge_exchange/briefing_
    papers/tomlinson110413.pdf
'31 July 1972': 'A Chronology of the Conflict', CAIN, Ulster
    University, http://cain.ulst.ac.uk/othelem/chron/ch72.htm
'a direct link between suicidal behaviour and having experienced
    a traumatic event': S. O'Neill et al., 'Patterns of Suicidal Ideation
    and Behavior in Northern Ireland and Associations with
    Conflict Related Trauma', PLoS One: 19 March 2014, https://doi.
    org/10.1371/journal.pone.0091532
'a study of Holocaust survivors': R. Yehuda et al., 'Holocaust
    Exposure Induced Intergenerational Effects on *FKBP5*
    Methylation', *Biological Psychiatry*, 12 August 2015,
    http://www.biologicalpsychiatryjournal.com/article/
    S0006-3223%2815%2900652-6/abstract

THE FIGHT OF YOUR LIFE

'modern interest in the disease has tended to veer towards
    the NFL': see David R. Weir, James S. Jackson and Amanda

Sonnega, 'Study of Retired NFL Players', University of Michigan, 10 September 2009, http://ns.umich.edu/Releases/2009/Sep09/FinalReport.pdf

'a New Jersey physican, Harrison Martland': https://www.ncbi.nlm.nih.gov/pubmed/7030057

'a 1928 journal article': Harrison Martland, 'Punch Drunk', 1928, https://jamanetwork.com/journals/jama/article-abstract/260461. See also the video clip of Dr Martland discussing the dangers of repeated blows to the head, 1948: http://www.gettyimages.co.uk/detail/video/chief-m-e-dr-harrison-s-martland-in-room-w-covered-news-footage/511634031

'a protein called tau, a common denominator in brain-related diseases': see papers by Ann McKee, Robert Stern and colleagues: 'Chronic Traumatic Encephalopathy in Athletes: Progressive Tauopathy Following Repetitive Head Injury', *Journal of Neuropathology & Experimental Neurology*, 68, issue 7 (July 2009), https://www.ncbi.nlm.nih.gov/pmc/articles/PMC2945234/; 'Clinical Presentation of Chronic Traumatic Encephalopathy', *Neurology*, 81 (21 August 2013), https://www.bu.edu/cte/files/2013/09/CTE-Neurology-2013-Stern-1122-9.pdf; 'Current Understanding of Chronic Traumatic Encephalopathy', *Current Treatment Options in Neurology*, 16 (2014), https://www.bu.edu/cte/files/2009/10/Baugh-CTE-review-2014.pdf

'Ann McKee arrives': Barbara Moran, 'Head Examiner', interview with Ann McKee, *The Brink*, Boston University, 12 February 2015, http://www.bu.edu/research/articles/head-examiner/

'Until they figure out how to diagnose CTE': consensus statement from the first National Institutes of Health consensus

conference on diagnosing CTE, https://www.ninds.nih.gov/
Current-Research/Focus-Research/Traumatic-Brain-Injury/
NIH-Chronic-Traumatic-Encephalopathy

BIGGER ISSUES THAN TRIBALISM BEING IGNORED AND NO ONE SEEMS TO CARE

'The reaction to Mike Nesbitt's vote transfer proposal': on 12
February 2017, Ulster Unionist leader Mike Nesbitt commented
on the *Sunday Politics* programme on BBC Northern Ireland
that he intended to give the SDLP his second preference vote in
the upcoming election

WANT A CAREER IN INVESTIGATIVE JOURNALISM? BECOME AN ENTREPRENEUR

'Musician Jerry Klickstein wrote a brilliant post': Jerry
Klickstein, 'Music Education and Entrepreneurship',
https://www.musiciansway.com/blog/2009/10/
music-education-and-entrepreneurship/

'When people backed Andrew Sullivan': Andrew Sullivan left the
Daily Beast to launch the *Daily Dish* as a standalone website
with subscribers

'Chris and Laura's story touched me': http://www.kickstarter.
com/projects/1368665357/a-one-year-student-reporting-lab-
within-homicide-w and http://contentsmagazine.com/articles/
homicide-watch-an-interview/

REQUIEM FOR A JOURNALIST

'I didn't know who Jaime Guadalupe González Domínguez was
until yesterday': Roy Greenslade, 'Mexican Online Journalist
Murdered', http://www.guardian.co.uk/media/greenslade/2013/
mar/05/journalist-safety-mexico

DECADES AFTER NORTHERN IRELAND'S 'TROUBLES', FAMILIES
OF THE DEAD ARE STILL SEEKING ANSWERS – AND TAKING THE
INVESTIGATIONS INTO THEIR OWN HANDS

'a three-month inquest into the shootings was set for September
2018': the inquest opened in November 2018. Its findings are
expected to be delivered in 2020.

HOW UNCOMFORTABLE CONVERSATIONS CAN SAVE LIVES

'This [48 per cent] is the percentage of trans youth alone in the
UK who have attempted suicide': figures taken from the Pace
survey in 2014, https://www.theguardian.com/society/2014/
nov/19/young-transgender-suicide-attempts-survey

Acknowledgements

'Progress' by Alan Gillis, from *Somebody, Somewhere* (2004), is reproduced by kind permission of the author and The Gallery Press. www.gallerypress.com

'Suicide of the Ceasefire Babies' (19 January 2016) and 'The Fight of Your Life' (22 November 2016) were first published by Wellcome on mosaicscience.com and are republished here under a Creative Commons licence.

'Why I Set Myself on Fire at Belfast City Hall – Man at Centre of Horrific Street Protest Breaks His Silence' (17 August 2015), 'The Ardoyne Festival Has Been Controversial at Times, But the Organiser Is Keen to Break Sectarian Barriers' (August 2015), 'Bigger Issues than Tribalism Being Ignored and No One Seems to Care' (18 February 2017), 'The Ceasefire Suicides' (14 April 2018), 'Fight for Equality Is as Much a Battle for Hearts and Minds as It Is for Legislation' (25 October 2016) and 'Tweet Suggests that LGBT People May Finally Have a Friend within the DUP' (7 August 2015) were first published in the *Belfast Telegraph* and are reproduced with permission.

'Want a Career in Investigative Journalism? Become an Entrepreneur', 'Requiem for a Journalist', 'A Letter to My Fourteen-Year-Old Self' and 'Picking the Right Stories to Investigate' were first published by *The Muckraker*, the investigative reporting website founded and edited by Lyra McKee.

Lyra McKee wrote about the legacy of the conflict known as the Troubles in her native Northern Ireland. This led her to investigate stories about mental health and suicide. She was also an advocate for LBGTQI+ rights. For further information or support see:

Samaritans (UK and ROI): tel. 116 123
www.samaritans.org

Switchboard LGBT+ helpline (UK): tel. 0300 330 0630
www.switchboard.lgbt

www.mind.org.uk

0141
249
0940 .